THE POWER
OF GOD
AT HOME

THE POWER
OF GOD
AT HOME

Nurturing Our Children
in Love and Grace

J. Bradley Wigger
Foreword by Mark Yaconelli

JOSSEY-BASS
A Wiley Imprint
www.josseybass.com

Jossey-Bass books and products are available through most bookstores. To contact
Jossey-Bass directly call our Customer Care Department within the U.S. at
800-956-7739, outside the U.S. at 317-572-3986 or fax 317-572-4002.

Jossey-Bass also publishes its books in a variety of electronic formats. Some content
that appears in print may not be available in electronic books.

Credits are on page 195.

Library of Congress Cataloging-in-Publication Data
Wigger, J. Bradley.
The power of God at home: nurturing our children in love and grace /
J. Bradley Wigger; foreword by Mark Yaconelli.—1st ed.
p. cm.—(The families and faith series)
Includes bibliographical references and index.
ISBN 0–7879–5588–4 (alk. paper)
1. Family—Religious life.   2. Parenting—Religious
aspects—Christianity.   I. Title.   II. Series.
BV4526.2 .W53 2003
248.8′45—dc21
2002012719

Printed in the United States of America
FIRST EDITION
HB Printing   10 9 8 7 6 5 4 3 2 1

THE FAMILIES AND FAITH SERIES

The Families and Faith Series is devoted to exploring the relationship between the spiritual life and our closest human relationships. From one generation to the next, faith and families are deeply intertwined in powerful ways. Faith puts all of life, including family life, in such a large perspective that it invites the gratitude, wonder, and hope so badly needed in the middle of the complexities and struggles of existence. On the other hand, faith becomes real only as it lives through concrete human relationships. Religion needs families and communities where the generations gather together and share and celebrate what it means to love God and to love others. At their best, faith and families are immersed in grace, and this series hopes to be a resource for those seeking to make love real in their families, congregations, and communities.

Diana R. Garland
> Director, Baylor Center for Family and Community Ministry
> Baylor University

J. Bradley Wigger
> Director, Center for Congregations and Family Ministries
> Louisville Presbyterian Theological Seminary

SERIES EDITORS

TITLES IN THE FAMILIES AND FAITH SERIES
Sacred Stories of Ordinary Families: Living the Faith in Daily Life
> Diana R. Garland
Let the Children Come: Reimagining Childhood from a Christian Perspective
> Bonnie J. Miller-McLemore
The Power of God at Home: Nurturing Our Children in Love and Grace
> J. Bradley Wigger
Seasons of a Family's Life: Cultivating the Contemplative Spirit at Home
> Wendy M. Wright

To David and Cora

CONTENTS

FOREWORD

The first conversation I had with Brad Wigger was during a conference on technology and religion. It was spring in Montana, and at the close of the day we decided to take a walk outside. As the sun set over the Clark Fork River, we began to share stories about the families we'd grown up in and the ways they shaped our faith and vocations. I remember Brad listened attentively as I talked about my own children and the struggles in providing meaningful experiences of faith for them. We walked on and fell silent as the sounds of the river mixed with the broad orange and purple tones of twilight around us. Then Brad began to tell me about a lake in Canada—a lake that his family took him to every summer as a boy. He told me how this place became a touchstone, a sacred retreat where he could measure and reflect on his life. He told me about the desire to provide this kind of ritual and tradition for his own children. We laughed as he told the stories of broken-down cars, all-night driving trips, and cranky children that came out of his hauling his family each summer from Kentucky to Canada. We paused and I watched a sense of wonder and gratitude come over him as he told me about watching his own kids swimming and fishing in the same lake at which he spent summers as a boy.

When I got home, I was eager to tell my wife about Brad and his family retreats to Canada. We began reflecting on our own family, about the schedule and rhythm of our own lives, and the rituals and pattern of life we were passing on to our children. It wasn't until later that I realized this was Brad's work: wondering at the mysteries of life, listening compassionately to the experiences of others, parenting with careful attentiveness to the needs of his children, creatively exploring the spiritual practices and rituals that enliven the soul, thinking deeply about what binds and frees the human spirit, sharing faithfully his gifts and wisdom with others, and returning again and again to the touchstones of the Christian faith. *The Power of God at Home* is a gift to congregations and communities of faith because it captures the same gentle wisdom, the same practical experience, and the same thoughtful attentiveness and inspiring questions that Brad graciously offered to me.

Brad Wigger has given us a book that most people in the church are looking for—a guide into the mysteries of family and God, children and church, and home and spirituality. Many of us who seek to live the Christian life harbor deep questions about family and religion. As a person who has spent fourteen years practicing, studying, and teaching youth ministry, I'm continually engaged in conversations with parents, grandparents, religious educators, and pastors about the correlation between family, church, and spiritual formation. In church parking lots and basements, in e-mail and airports, parents and church leaders pull me aside to ask questions that keep them up at night: "Do you pray with your kids?" "Should I make my son go to church?" "Shouldn't I let my daughter find her own spiritual path?"

These are not the questions that are addressed by parenting manuals and how-to books. Yet they are the questions that Brad tenderly opens up for reflection and wonder. As the director of the Center for Congregations and Family Ministries at Louisville Seminary, Brad is uniquely qualified to discuss and reflect on the deep tensions and possibilities for family and religion. Yet this book does not come from a lectern or a pulpit. It does not come from an "expert." It comes from the heart of a committed parent, seeker, and teacher who hopes to awaken others to the sacred dimension of daily life.

With clear and compelling descriptions, Brad makes available a rich set of resources within the Christian tradition, the Bible, and communities of faith that strengthen the sacred rhythms of family and religion. He provides a theological and biblical primer that many of us within the church have looked for as we seek to be teachers and spiritual guides for our children. He helps us recognize simple practices of faith that can be realized within our families and congregations. And yet Brad also understands the harried and addictive culture in which families seek to shelter faith. He names the cycles of dissatisfaction and meaninglessness, the spiritual vacancy and homelessness that many of us experience in our consumer culture. He maps the subterranean desires, fears and hopes, sin and grace that can deepen or damage our family and communal relationships.

Brad has succeeded in creating a work that will benefit pastors, parents, Christian educators, church members, and youth ministers. It is a book that is needed in adult education programs, parenting groups, and seminary classrooms. It is a book I will recommend to the hundreds of parents and church leaders I meet each year who are wondering about their roles in the spiritual lives of their children. Just as if they were walking with a good spiritual teacher, those who read this work will emerge encouraged, less burdened, and more aware of the availability of God within their own families and congregations.

"I would like to see home and family life reclaimed as spiritual territory." This is not just Brad's hope but also the yearning of the coming generations. It is the longing of the children and young people that I know and work with. If we're honest, this is also the persistent desire within our own hearts that home might be a place of rest and celebration, of meaning and deep connection, of creativity and acceptance, and of real commitment and spontaneous laughter. May Brad inspire you as he inspired me to continue reflecting about the mystery of God and the rhythms of family life. And may this book reveal to you as it has revealed to me all the love and grace that is available within the places we call home.

Mark Yaconelli
Coauthor, *Way to Live: Practicing Our Faith with Youth*

ACKNOWLEDGMENTS

I am deeply grateful to many friends and colleagues who read early drafts of selected chapters, provided helpful feedback, and heaped support and ideas upon me and the project generally. Thanks go to Eugene March, Chip and Linda Andrus, Sally Bull, Sheri Ferguson, Tim Shapiro, Tim Hoyt-Duncan, Judd Hendrix, Carol Cook, Lynn Roberson, David Wood, John M. Mulder, Carla and David Cousley, Sherrie Schork, Michelle Melton, Laura March, John McClure, Edie Luther, and Shandra Daniels.

I am particularly indebted to the editors involved: to the late Sarah Polster, whose idea it was for the *Families and Faith Series* and who is terribly missed, and to Sheryl Fullerton and Julianna Gustafson at Jossey-Bass who, remarkably, stepped up to continue the project. I am thankful beyond words to Diana R. Garland, who supported, edited, and encouraged this work at every stage. What a friend!

I am thankful to Louisville Presbyterian Theological Seminary for granting me sabbatical leave for writing this book and to the Lilly Endowment, particularly Chris Coble and Craig Dykstra, for a grant supporting the leave and supporting the book series.

My family has been deeply involved in this book. Not only have they created many of the experiences shared here in the first place (and allowed me to share them), they read portions of the book and listened to me talk about it beyond any reasonable level. Grace abounds through them. Thank you Mom and Dad (Jim and Emily

Wigger), MeMe (Cora Nell Simpson), and John and Kim Wigger. Jane, David, and Cora—what can I say? You are radically amazing, not only blessing me but so many others. Thank you.

INTRODUCTION

It was a tough time. Right out of college, with my degree in social work, I went to a seminary—a place primarily devoted to training ministers. However, I soon discovered that I wasn't so sure it was the place for me. I was depressed, scared, and overwhelmed by the academic and professional expectations. I let it slip that I was thinking of leaving, and some wonderful people rallied, encouraging me to hang in there. But somehow the encouragement backfired, intensifying the expectations, making matters worse. Then I spoke with my folks, who were as eager as any parents to see their son do well in school. They listened carefully and offered these simple words: "Well, you know you always have a place here."

It was grace. They would support me whichever way I went and give me a place to figure it out if I needed it. The load was gone. I knew about theological grace. I knew that we don't earn God's love; it is already there. But this event gave it new texture. At that moment, God's grace was beaming through the love of my parents. I stayed in school, but that is not the point. I could have left, could have done something else. But having a place, an actual place, a place in my heart, a place with God even, freed me to actually enjoy the experience of being in seminary. I was free to learn, to work hard, to play, to make some of the best friends ever, and even to fall in love. It was a good time.

The seeds of those words from my parents meaning anything constructive to me were sown in my childhood. For some, such words from their parents might have no impact, or the impact might even be negative. The "place" they know is not so gracious, the seeds bad. My work in congregations and in social service agencies has made it clear to me that families can curse children as well as bless them. Most of the time, like any human relationship, families are a mixture of good and bad. Mine certainly is, but so are the families of the Bible. Perfect parenting is not the goal of the Bible or of this book. However, the Bible does let us know that homes, even in the midst of their flaws, can be places of blessing. Gracious moments, security, creative living, teaching and learning, play, commitments, service, care, and more are windows to an Eternal Love that holds us tight and won't let go. Families and homes can reveal grace.

So this book is for those who like windows in their homes; it is for parents, particularly, or for those working with parents or children in congregations. It is for those who hope homes can be places where children will see God's love and know it deeply. I do not assume or believe that to be a family there must be children, but this book is about families that do have children at home. I also know that parents do not always come in pairs, and when they do, they may not agree on everything religious. But I am writing for homes that are at least faith-friendly, even if there are doctrinal differences. My conviction is that everyday life, including home life, is one of the most important teachers in children's lives. And one of the most important lessons young people can learn is that they are children of God.

Through this book, I share some stories from my own family life with children because these are some of the windows to grace that I know best. I am very grateful to Jane, David, and Cora for letting me share them, because this means strangers see through the glass into our home as well, and that can be a little unnerving. As a fellow parent, however, I could not imagine reading a book about family life and parenting without some glimpses into the author's own experiences. But just remember, they are only glimpses. We are probably both more loving and more nasty, more fun and more boring, at times, than these glimpses reveal. My larger hope is that, through the stories and the subject matter, parents will take a second look at their own homes, their own faith, and what they have to do with one another.

One of the best ways to see the connections between faith and our own everyday lives is to spend time with the Bible. Scripture lets us see through the windows to grace that our ancient ancestors knew and celebrated. So this book spends some time considering the power of home and family life in the story of faith told through the Bible. As is true for most homes, it is a story full of ups and downs, frustrations and joys, tragedies and redemption. Ultimately, the Bible is a love story—an account of God's passionate love for this world that in turn roots our own loves and stories and passions in the power of grace.

I now teach at that school where I first struggled twenty years ago, Louisville Presbyterian Seminary. I teach religious education and direct the seminary's Center for Congregations and Family Ministries. The creation of the Center is deeply relevant to the concerns of this book. Presbyterians, like many mainstream religious denominations, have suffered massive losses in membership in the last thirty to forty years. The seminary engaged in a major research project in the late 1980s to explore this situation. The reasons for the loss are complex and multiple, but a contributing factor has to do with families. By and large, the home is losing its place and power in the life of faith. Over time, children seem to be learning less and less about anything religious at home. Congregations, more and more, are expected to handle this kind of teaching. Parents and congregational leaders, curriculum materials, and seminary courses in education increasingly have all come to treat the congregation and its classrooms as the context for spiritual learning. And it certainly is, but it is not the only context. In Protestant history, the home was considered "the cradle of faith" and even "a little seminary." In Judaism, the dinner table, from weekly *Shabbat* to Passover, has been essential to nurturing religious learning and practice in each generation. The Catholic and Evangelical worlds have seen families in similar ways, but all are struggling to sustain this vision. So the Center was established to begin exploring ways in which home and family life, in conjunction with congregational life, can re-enter the religious and educational imaginations of congregational leaders and seminarians.

Through this book, I hope to encourage parents to enter the exploration as well. They—you—are the most important factor. No one is more important to your children.

THE POWER
OF GOD
AT HOME

Chapter 1

PAYING ATTENTION

The Spiritual Power of Learning

Our first summer together, when Jane and I were newly married, we drove from our apartment in Denver across the plains of eastern Colorado and on to Kansas. I grew up near St. Louis, on the Mississippi River, with all its bluffs and hills as well as trees and humidity, so I was not accustomed to such flat land, such dry heat, or such distance between service stations. I began calculating how many marathons I would have to run to get help if our old Mazda broke down out there—a real possibility. As we crossed the border into western Kansas, I felt a strange combination of boredom and panic. The landscape was mind-numbing by then, and the gas gauge was getting a little too low. I looked at Jane, and she had a glaze in her eyes that I first attributed to highway hypnosis, but when I saw her slight smile I knew she was thinking something good.

"Isn't it beautiful?" she more proclaimed than asked.

"What?"

"Here."

"Where?"

"Here, this place," she answered.

Though we were in the same place, I knew we were in different worlds. So I asked, "What do you see?"

She said, "Home."

Jane began teaching me about her home. She pointed to the huge sky and its colors, the fields of wheat and its readiness for harvest, the trees and the windbreaks, the wind blowing through the wild grasses, and the combines and silos and snow fences. These observations spilled into stories of growing up on these plains and what it meant to live in a farm town, and I began to see Jane in a fuller way. I got to know her a little better that afternoon. I learned.

SEEING IN DEPTH

My job is to teach congregational leaders about learning and teaching, that is, to prepare them to be teachers themselves and to plan for educational ministries. I love classroom teaching, and I want my students to love being teachers, too. But as a place of learning, the classroom is extremely limited, and if our imaginations for teaching and learning are locked into the classroom, our imaginations for education become extremely limited as well. We miss so much, including the ways in which children and adults alike learn in the midst of everyday family life. Our home and family life are places of learning. They are certainly much more; they mean much more and involve much more. But they are, nonetheless, very powerful places of learning. They are contexts for spiritual learning, even though parents are often very intimidated by this idea, just as my students are intimidated by the prospect of being spiritual teachers and leaders.

One task that helps education students begin to gain confidence and facility as teachers is to pay attention to learning itself. What is learning? How does it happen? Where does it take place? What cultivates an atmosphere for learning? How does it affect someone to learn something new? Questions like this can help us pay attention. Learning happens all around us and in us and through us. So when it comes to appreciating the ways in which home and family life play a role in spiritual learning, it helps to pay attention to how any kind of learning happens. Learning involves seeing things in a deeper way. Driving across Kansas, not only did I see Jane in a fuller way but I saw the landscape with a newly appreciated depth. Of course, the depth was there all along; I simply noticed aspects of the landscape I had previously missed. A lot of learning is like this—a matter of taking the time and energy to notice what is before our very eyes. And this is true of learning about learning itself.

Seeing with depth, appreciating newly discovered dimensions of life—that is, learning—is an important part of the spiritual life. Learning, in the context of faith, involves seeing the world, seeing one another, and even seeing ourselves in ever fuller ways. Spiritual learning involves paying attention to the sacred. The sacred also has depth that can be appreciated, known, and celebrated. There is a loving grace at work all around us and in us and through us, even in our own homes. Religious education is about seeing this love and living by it.

There are certainly things we can do as parents to help cultivate this vision for ourselves and for our children. For example, patterns of life, regular rituals, and faith-oriented activities all help. This is to say that religious practice is critical to religious learning. Home is the kind of place that lets children learn by doing things with us, from cooking to gardening to praying, and learn from us, even as we can learn from them. I will talk more about the role that religious activities such as praying or scripture reading play in family life later in the book, in very concrete ways, because children and parents benefit powerfully from these practices. But I want to establish a larger point first: apart from a larger vision of meaning, apart from a deeper glimpse into the nature and power of faith itself, even prayer or reading the Bible can quickly lose meaning and power.

Frankly, there are tons of books and other materials on the market that tell parents exactly what they should be doing. These deal in a kind of technology—the technology of parenting: how to get children to sleep through the night, how to make them behave, how to give them good self-esteem, even how to make them spiritual. Such how-to helps can be a great resource to parents (Who could be against getting kids to sleep?), and I have used some of them gratefully. However, I must admit that these materials affect me in another way, too. Every time I see a news story, book, television spot, or radio show telling me what I should be doing to be a better parent, I feel a bit resentful. It's one more doggone thing that I need to do or that I'm doing wrong or that I've failed at as a parent. In fact, sometimes these how-tos do just the opposite of what they are supposed to do. Instead of giving parents resources and empowering them, they make us feel stupid and guilty. Of course, there are certainly things to learn how to do, as a parent, or how to do better, but saturation in these kinds of messages can actually be disempowering, as they continually communicate that experts and professionals manage their lives (and children) so much better than the rest of us poor, hapless parents.

My hope is that this book will work in a different direction. This book offers a chance to ponder other kinds of questions, beyond the how-to variety. The spiritual life has always taken other kinds of questions seriously—questions like these:

Who is God?

Who is my neighbor?

Where does evil come from?

Where should we worship?

Why should we care?

What is faith?

Why is love so difficult at times?

These are the kinds of questions, as they are explored, that provide the deeper background to the activities and rituals of the spiritual life. They are the kinds of issues, when wrestled with, that yield meaning to the things we do. Good questions help us pay attention. Although raising children is a deep source of joy and love, it is also very demanding work. Nothing sustains hard work better than a sense of meaning in it. Likewise, nothing sustains the harder works of faith better than a sense of meaning in them. In the end, how-to questions are indeed important; so are why and where and who questions. The hope is that we can learn from them all and see our lives in deep and meaningful ways. Maybe our children can, too.

THE RELATIONSHIP BETWEEN ATTENTION AND MEANING

As Jane told me stories, as she pointed to features of "home," I was able to see things that had previously been veiled or part of a vague background. She helped me pay attention. Learning and paying attention are so intertwined that it is difficult to tell where one ends and the other begins. Again, learning happens all around us, so one of the best ways to learn about learning is to notice it. How have you learned? How do your children learn? What seems to be going on? What are some of the key ingredients? How does this particular child seem to pick up things? How does that one? It may seem a slightly odd way of putting it, but the best teachers are the ones who become connoisseurs, in a sense, of learning. Educational connoisseurs (good teachers) are able to appreciate aspects and dimensions of learning others easily miss. A connoisseur, in this sense, is someone who has learned enough about something to attend to subtleties and nuances that most people cannot sense. It could be wine, but it could be baseball, jazz, or antiques. The connoisseur appreciates the qualities that make this particular thing different from or similar to everything else.

In this way, Jane, compared to me, is a connoisseur of western Kansas. Her time living there, her experiences, and her history form a rich background that allows her to attend to qualities of Kansas that I would miss. Or consider baseball. The larger background of baseball allows the baseball connoisseur (or good fan) to appreciate this particular game, with the St. Louis Cardinals, who are two runs down, with bases loaded, in the bottom of the ninth, a 3-2 count, two outs, a wild card spot on the line, and Mark McGuire batting. To someone unfamiliar with baseball, this situation means nothing. The next pitch matters not. But at the game in St. Louis, the next pitch will hold the attention of fifty thousand people. The context—the larger backdrop of baseball—helps the connoisseur or fan know how meaningful the next pitch is.

The point is that the ability to pay attention happens in relation to a larger context of meaning. Learning, spiritual or otherwise, involves seeing a particular part in relation to a greater whole. This is a basic educational principle because the relationship between part and whole affects how we see. The background in a picture affects the foreground; a musical composition affects each note; words take on meaning by their contexts, letters by their words. The letter *A,* for example, only makes sense within a larger alphabet; that alphabet makes sense within the English language, which itself has a larger history. A child may learn to recognize the letter *A,* distinguishing it from other letters. But that is only the first step. The goal is to be able to say it, write it, and see it in relation to other letters and words. As this happens, the letter *A* becomes increasingly meaningful; *A* is a letter, a vowel, a word, an article, a sound, or maybe an initial. Learning happens by paying attention to the relationship between parts and wholes, and the result is meaning.

The relationship between part and whole is not only relevant to baseball or learning language skills, it is relevant to family life as well. Driving across Kansas, I learned about Jane; I saw her more clearly as I saw her home and heard more stories from her background. She has learned a lot about me in the same way: hearing stories, seeing my home, getting to know my family of origin better and better, and even by hearing stories from my family tree about ancestors that neither she nor I ever met. But then, as we have shared and continue to share new experiences (like driving across Kansas together), more and more our individual lives (parts) become meaningful in light of our relationship (a larger whole). In other words, attention and meaning support each other. Meaning helps us attend to subtleties and deeper dimensions of life, but as we pay attention, these subtleties and dimensions often become more meaningful.

LEARNING WHO WE ARE

The relationship between part and whole is not only fundamental to learning, to attention, and to meaning, it is fundamental to knowing who we are. The relationship is crucial to identity. Children learn who they are—even *that* they are—in relationship to a larger context of families, caregivers, and friends, for example. It is easy to forget that, at some point, children even have to learn their own names. Our names themselves—usually a combination of family names and newly chosen ones for this particular child (which, too, are often ancestral names)—reveal how children gain their identities in relation to a larger context.

When our daughter Cora (named for her great-grandmother) was first learning words, we played a little game at the dinner table that let her practice with our names, as well as hers:

"Cora, can you say, 'Daddy'?"

She would respond, "Dah-dah."

"Can you say, 'Mommy'?" "Mah-mah."

"Can you say, 'David'?" "Day-day."

"Can you say, 'Cora'?" She responded, "Co-wah."

Every night for a good week or so, Cora would respond the same way, repeating the names, including her own. Then a change occurred.

"Cora, can you say, 'Daddy'?" and so forth. She repeated our names. But when we came to the question, "Can you say 'Cora'?" she looked puzzled and said nothing. It was if her words were paralyzed. For several days, she continued to repeat our names as before, but when it came to her own, she offered only silence. Then another shift occurred.

"Cora, can you say, 'Daddy'?" "Dah-dah."

"Can you say, 'Mommy'?" "Mah-mah."

"Can you say, 'David'?" "Day-day."

"Can you say, 'Cora'?" This time she smiled and declared, "Me!"

At this point, her name was not just a name for her to repeat; nor was her name a word she simply responded to if we used it. Now these parts were connected in a meaningful way in "me." What begins as learning one's name continues in various ways for the rest of life. We learn who we are in relation to others, in relation to our families, in relation to our ancestors, in relation to a larger community. Critically, however, children are not simply products of their parents, families, and communities; children affect them all as well. Parts can change the whole, and children do so all the time. Jane and I have been learning a lot about who we are as we raise our little "me's" and as they raise us.

There are spiritual implications here. The relationship between part and whole is not only a fundamental principle for understanding how learning happens and not only fundamental for understanding how a child's identity emerges but this principle is fundamental to appreciating why faith matters. The sixteenth-century theologian John Calvin put it this way: "Without knowledge of God there is no knowledge of self." In other words, according to Calvin, the self, the part, is seen in light of the largest whole, God. Ultimately, from this point of view, our identities are actually spiritual identities. Our ultimate roots are in God. Yet Calvin reversed the statement too, saying, "Without knowledge of self, there is no knowledge of God." Again, each part matters to the whole. Knowledge of the self even reveals something about God. Our own stories, experiences, history, struggles, and joys, for example, potentially put us in touch with our ultimate roots. Our lives, including our family lives, are sources of sacred knowledge. But it takes the eyes to see our family lives this way. It takes vision.

Putting these pieces of learning together, we could say then that when our lives, including our families, homes, and children, are viewed against their larger, sacred context, these parts of our lives become more meaningful. And we could say that as the larger, sacred context is viewed in relation to the parts of our lives, faith itself becomes more meaningful.

THE POSSIBILITIES OF LEARNING

The little name game with Cora happened to catch a transition in her life and reveals the possibilities that emerge when learning happens. The ability to repeat her name eventually led the way for her to represent herself to herself. When this happens for children, it is a genuine mental leap. And with the leap comes new possibilities. This is what learning does; it generates possibilities, including the possibility of knowing who we are in deeper ways.

In one sense, children learn just like other creatures. Children learn to communicate, walk, eat, and play, for example, just as birds learn to fly, bear cubs learn to climb trees, and ducklings learn to swim. But when it comes to the human creature, learning takes on a whole new range of possibilities. Babbling opens the way to words, to reading and writing, to singing, to novels, to speeches, to opera, to mass communication. We are even sending messages into outer space, wondering if they will be received by anything that can communicate back. Crawling, in children, opens the way to walking, running, traveling, doing gymnastics, dancing ballet, excelling at athletics, and more. Learning is not only a matter of practicalities but of possibilities. Consider learning particle physics or an ancient language. Consider learning jazz guitar or the history of China. Or consider learning to perform micro-surgery on neonates. Who knows what people might be learning a thousand years from now? Thirty thousand years from now? The possibilities are dizzying. Learning in human beings is wonderfully strange. It may begin with basic survival skills, but it is also complex and open-ended, just as we are. There is always more to learn, and this is as true in the spiritual life as it is with any other kind of learning.

Following Cora's leap into "me," a new possibility emerged. She could say no. She, as well as her parents, started saying no a lot more often. (Perhaps you have seen the T-shirt, just the right size for a toddler, that reads, "I think my name is 'No.'") Why are "me" and "no" connected? Once Cora could represent herself to herself, she could imagine herself in new ways, and this included the possibility of not doing what we expected. "Me" represents the birth of choice and, with it, individuality. And as frustrating as this new world of possibility is to a parent, we would not want our children unable to say no in this troubled world. It is going to come in very handy. Saying no is critical for children, but they have to practice on those they trust will love them, even when they are contrary.

Like many parents, Jane and I began using reverse logic tricks we had learned from our own parents in the midst of these little rebellions. "Whatever you do, don't you dare eat your oatmeal," we'd say. And of course our kids would delight in eating their oatmeal.

"Don't you put your pajamas on right now." And pretty soon they were ready for bed. (By the way, I once made the mistake of trying this with someone else's child, and it only confused and scared him. He didn't know me well enough to oppose me.) Eventually, kids catch on and it doesn't work any longer, but even so, I remember Cora, particularly, saying to Jane or me, "Tell me not to eat my apple." "Cora, don't you dare eat that apple." And she would smile all the way through it. Everything a child learns opens the door to more possibilities.

So, what wonderfully strange creatures we are. We can take our instincts and soar with them. We can search the stars for life; we can make marvelous music; we can explore our history to the beginning of the universe. The possibilities are endless. So much is this kind of possibility a part of human existence that we need ways of expressing this wonder. Humanity learns to create art, engaging our imaginations and senses with beauty. Therefore, when a child learns "me," it is only the beginning of the child's learning who he or she is. We are creatures, in the poetry of Psalm 8 of the Bible, made only a little lower than God, crowned with glory and honor.

OVERWHELMING POSSIBILITIES

There is another side to possibility. The writer Anne Lamott tells the story of her brother becoming overwhelmed by a homework assignment that he had put off too long. He was ten years old and trying to write a report on birds that he'd put off for three months. With his paper due the next day, "he was at the kitchen table close to tears, surrounded by binder paper and pencils and unopened books on birds, immobilized by the hugeness of the task ahead." Their father, also a writer, knew something about being overwhelmed by large tasks (like writing a novel) and gave his son some helpful advice. He "sat down beside him, put his arm around my brother's shoulder, and said, 'Bird by bird, buddy. Just take it bird by bird.'"

Our wonderfully strange nature has its own difficulties. The world of possibilities opens onto a world of responsibilities. We can choose not to do our homework or to put it off. Or even if we decide to do it, we can become overwhelmed by the immensity of the task. The world of possibilities opens the way to anxiety, bad choices, or irresponsibility. The same freedom that allows a child to say "me" or to ask, "What should I do about this homework?" allows that child to eventually ponder such adult questions as "Who am I?" and "What should I do with my life?" Although the great breadth of possibilities can be exciting, at the same time it creates the kind of choices that weigh heavily on our shoulders. What's the right thing to do? What's the wrong? Is there a right and a wrong in this situation? Moral dilemmas are born in the awareness of possibilities, and finding good guidance is not always so easy.

So learning not only generates possibilities but possibilities generate dilemmas. Should we get married? Is it time for children? Should we move? Should I go back to school? These possibilities can create a lot of stress and anxiety because the stakes are high. Should I have the surgery? Am I willing to die for this cause or this country? What do we value? How do I know? Whom do I trust? These are some of the big questions that people face in life. And when we find ourselves deeply entangled with the lives of others—close friends, relatives, work colleagues, couples, or spouses, for example—the possibilities multiply and the responsibility intensifies. We have to make decisions in relationship with others. Once children can say "me," once they say "no," once their budding individuality emerges, they also have to learn how to negotiate "me" in relation to others. Saying no may have consequences for others. "Me" and "no" are only the beginning of learning something that they will have to negotiate the rest of their lives.

Parenting complicates matters further. The younger children are, the more parents are making decisions for them, from when bedtime is to what town to live in. Some decisions are routine; some are life-shaping. What time do we eat? Who does what around the house? How do we spend money? How do we treat others? What do we believe about God? How does God relate to how we spend money or treat others? But then, as children grow, so grows their own capacity for freedom, responsibility, and possibility. Not only do they need to know "me" but they need to know "you." Not only do they need to be able to stand up for themselves or say no to temptations or harm, they also need to be able to respect others, to say yes to good things, and live in community with others. In the end, our children may well make decisions for us one day, so the entanglement thickens.

One of the hopes for the spiritual life is that, through it, not only do we learn and find meaning but we can find some guidance as well—guidance for ourselves as parents but also a guidance that our children can learn and rely on when we are not around. In the spiritual life, such guidance in the face of life's possibilities is called wisdom. The hope is that the spiritual life can help us be wiser parents and that our children can themselves grow in wisdom. Wisdom guides; wisdom generates possibilities. Although the wonderful side of our nature needs beauty and freedom to thrive, the strange side needs direction and guidance. The task of raising children makes this very clear. Children need freedom and choices to open the way to discovering the wonders of existence, including the beauty of their own lives. But children also need down-to-earth guidance and a wise hand to lead them through the dangers and responsibilities of living. The hope that guides spiritual learning, then, is that wisdom is possible.

The writer Norman Maclean puts it more gracefully and bluntly in his story *A River Runs Through It*. The story is about growing up and fly-fishing in Montana. Norman Maclean is the son of a minister, and he writes of his father's view of human nature. "As a Scot and a Presbyterian, my father believed that man by nature was a mess and had fallen from an original state of grace. Somehow, I developed early the notion that he did this by falling from a tree." In the movie based on the book, there is a kind of visual representation of the tangled mess of human nature. One of the boys, while out fly-fishing, gets his line all caught up in a bush behind him. This preacher's son explains, "Until man is redeemed he will always take a fly rod too far back, just as natural man always overswings with an ax or golf club and loses all his power somewhere in the air; only with a rod it's worse, because the fly often comes so far back it gets caught in a bush or rock."

For some, this is too pessimistic; for others not enough so. But it does get at our complicated nature and our need for help. For Maclean this help, this redemption, is a religious matter. But just as good fly-casting has its own grace and rhythms, Maclean learned from his father that "only by picking up God's rhythms were we able to regain power and beauty." Spiritual learning is about picking up God's rhythms. These rhythms are patterns of grace that redeem the chaos and trouble that can plague our complex, overwhelming lives.

UNDERSTANDING POWER AND BEAUTY

Power, in our mechanistic age, is associated with the ability to control things. Beauty, in our electronic age, is associated with skin-deep screen images. The power and beauty of the religious life are of a different order. In fact, faith reveals the ultimate ugliness of the kind of power that thrives on control. By overswinging, as Maclean puts it, we lose power, and this is as true in family life as anywhere else. Overswinging works about as well in home life as it does in fly-fishing or golf, but it is more dangerous. As a social worker, I saw the tragic results of parents' vain and futile attempts to use force to regain power. It inevitably fails. It is unwise. (Our instincts gave us the capacity to fight in order to defend ourselves against predators, not to control children or turn on spouses.) Instead, the religious life and the life of learning are after the kind of power that respects the dignity of others, that sees the wonder of their lives, and that is guided by the wisdom of faith. This kind of power is real and enduring.

Not only are families tempted to overswing but religion itself and learning as well can fall from the tree and make a mess. On the one hand, if our religion is too small, it easily shrinks into a closed little cult; if our god is too narrow, it resists loving others outside the circle; if our learning is too limited, it will not endure the complexities of our living. On the other hand, there is a long and ancient history of people discovering a God whose power works in a larger direction—a God who frees people, who loves, who redeems in the midst of ugliness. This long and ancient history of faith is critical to spiritual learning, as it continually reveals God's rhythms. This is why the Bible is so important, why scriptures are sacred as they are read and studied and prayed. As people pick up these rhythms, they discover grace happening in their own lives—a grace that gives power and beauty a chance to thrive, even in the mess of human affairs.

A contemporary illustration of this ancient power comes through the true story of Ruby Bridges. Her story has been documented by Harvard psychiatrist Robert Coles, not to mention the newspapers and Norman Rockwell's famous painting of a young girl in pigtails being escorted by federal agents. Ruby was six years old in 1960 when she became the first black child to be sent to the first grade of a white New Orleans public school. Day after day, this tiny six-year-old girl faced a white mob with their ugly signs and venomous shouts, and she walked on through them and into a classroom where she was the only student. The other parents had pulled their children out of school. This happened week after week for nearly the entire school year.

Coles, as he first witnessed all of this, was amazed and somewhat perplexed by this little girl. On the one hand, she would draw pictures of herself in which she subconsciously (according to Coles) revealed how frail and vulnerable she was compared to the powerful, threatening white world around her. On the other hand, there she was, walking through the crowd tall and courageous. Her strength seemed larger than an individual child should have. Coles says that he just didn't get it.

But a few years ago, Coles wrote a children's book about Ruby in which he tells the story for children and along the way reveals that he finally got it; through the story, he helps us get it too. Before that first day of school, the family went to church as usual. The children's book shows the family sitting in a pew. The children's hands are folded; Ruby's father's head is bowed; her mother has her head and hands up. As Ruby's mother reports it, "We sat there and prayed to God, that we'd all be strong and we'd have courage and we'd get through any trouble; and Ruby would be a good girl and she'd hold her head up high. We prayed long and we prayed hard," says her mother in the book. Indeed, there was more than an individual little girl walking through that crowd; there was a family, a congregation, a people, a Spirit moving like Moses and the Israelites through the Red Sea.

THE POWER OF GOD AT HOME

As if this story were not powerful enough, one day Ruby's teacher looked out the window and saw her talking to the crowd. The teacher, surprised and worried, asked her about this when Ruby got to the room. Ruby replied, "I wasn't talking," she said. "I was praying." She was asking God to forgive these people.

It turns out that Ruby would always stop and pray a few blocks before she got to school, but on this morning she had forgotten until she came upon the crowd. So she prayed in the middle of it.

In the children's book, Ruby's act of praying for this mob of people is clearly connected to the story of the crucifixion of Jesus in the gospel according to Luke, a story Ruby knows and draws upon in this terrible situation. People—leaders and soldiers—are scoffing at Jesus on the cross.

> When they came to the place that is called The Skull, they crucified Jesus there with the criminals, one on his right and one on his left. Then Jesus said, "Father, forgive them; for they do not know what they are doing" [Luke 23:33–34].

Coles, in this simple children's book, reveals spiritual power. The power is deeply connected to Ruby's family, to their faith, to the larger congregation, to a community, to a history of faith. All of these, especially as they work together, are critical to picking up God's rhythms. The story of Ruby going to school is a particularly dramatic one. We hope that none of our children will face such challenging circumstances in their lives, but inevitably some will. In addition to being inspiring, the story demonstrates how faith can matter in personal and public realms alike. It demonstrates the difference between the kind of ugly power that overswings and the spiritual power that redeems with grace. Ruby's story illustrates the power and beauty of religious learning and practice, at home, in congregations, and in public life.

EMPOWERING PARENTS

If home life is critical to learning who we are and is indeed a cradle of faith, then it would be dangerous to forget about the role of parents in the spiritual lives of children. But when it comes to parents, many congregations are stuck in a vicious cycle. The more we expect congregations to handle spiritual nurture, the less parents see themselves as religious teachers or their homes as spiritual territory and, in turn, the more we expect of congregations.

I asked a group of parents in a church once: "What if I suggested that you are spiritual teachers for your children? What would your reaction be?" Most of the parents cringed, or squirmed, or tried to avoid eye contact. And for a long time no one said a word. Finally, a mother boldly spoke up. She said, "My first reaction is, 'No way! I'm not qualified.' But then I realized, 'I am a spiritual teacher for your child, and yours, and yours [she pointed around the room]. I teach them all in Sunday School.'"

As we expect more of the congregation, not only are its professionals busier and busier, so are lay people, often parents, attending committee meetings, teaching classes, running programs, or serving search committees seeking new and improved professionals to meet the ever-expanding expectations of ministry. Meanwhile, home gets left in the spiritual dust, a ghost town for faith. This only intensifies parents' own sense of inadequacy. Tragically, children, in turn, learn what they live—a sense of spiritual inferiority. This is the vicious cycle.

Through my work with the Center and seminary, I have also discovered many, many parents who hope for something different. And I have discovered congregational leaders who are working in a different direction, that is, in the direction of empowering parents. These parents themselves are looking for help, for resources, and for sources of wisdom in their overwhelming task of raising children. They are not just looking for another program to get their kids into; many already have enough of those. These parents want their children to know that home is spiritual territory too, even if these parents are not totally sure what that means. Because just as saying no is first tried out on those a child can trust, saying "God" may be too; many parents, at a gut level, know this and want their children to learn who they are in relation to God.

Not all parents, of course, are this motivated. Spirituality may be more like a gentle tugging. Some new parents realize that even though they are not sure what they even believe anymore, they want their child to have some kind of exposure to the religious life. Other parents grew up with "nothing," as they put it, and want "something more" for their own children. Still others found their own religious upbringing oppressive or anything but gracious, yet they cannot throw their own baby out with this spiritual bath water. Then again, some parents have always held their faith as important, have always expected to practice faith as a family; they too can be caught off guard by the new responsibility they feel or the simple but profound questions children can pose. Sometimes these parents feel it worse. They feel they should be doing something, but they are not sure what; they feel the Bible is important, but they don't know it very well; they feel that they should pray more, but they are not sure what to say.

Now here is the dilemma. The very open-ended nature of learning combines with the eternally deep subject of God to make matters all the more overwhelming to parents. There are people around who seem to know an awful lot about spiritual things. People can spend their lifetimes struggling with questions like these:

What happens when we die?

Who is God?

Why do bad things happen?

So when our children ask such questions, how the heck am I supposed to answer them? There are folk who have spent years learning the Bible, the original biblical languages such as Hebrew and Greek, and three more ancient near-Eastern languages that shed light on how to translate the word *justice* in its original context. So who am I to try to teach my kids anything religious? Some reticence in thinking of oneself as a spiritual teacher seems warranted. It can be a sign of respect for the subject matter and for all the scholarship around it. And that is the dilemma. The same rigorous academic standards that have improved the quality of theological scholarship and religious study in the mainstream religious world also increase the sense of inadequacy among those who have not received such training.

Yet even highly trained religious educators, clergy, scholars, and professors can be at a loss as to how to render, to their own children, the theological complexities they have spent years studying. More than once, our own children have said something like the following to Jane (a pastor and teacher) or me, as we struggled out a long answer to a religious question: "Uh, I don't know what you just said, but I was just trying to remember the town where Jesus was born." Or the hands go up into the stop position: "That's okay, I'll just ask my Sunday school teacher." So whether it is a sense of inadequacy born of too little knowledge or a sense of frustration born of too much information, teaching our children raises some important challenges.

Therefore, in an atmosphere where we expect congregations to handle more and more, the great danger is that we, as parents, will run from the challenge. Oddly enough, an unintended danger beneath our own religious education programs and classrooms is that it may make running from the challenge easier. In fact, in the nineteenth century, huge debates raged in the Protestant world concerning whether or not this new development, the Sunday school, was a good thing. What was the problem? Religious leaders worried that the Sunday school was usurping the role of parents and families. This, in turn, was contributing to a decline in "family religion" (devotions, prayer, worship, instruction), according to some. Others argued back that among families whose children were in Sunday school, there was actually greater engagement in family religion. (This is the direction in which I lean.) But the debate itself reveals the danger. Congregational programs and schools can disable the role of parents if they are not careful. Or maybe the greater danger is when this debate doesn't occur to anyone anymore because the role of home in spiritual nurture has been lost.

The dilemma is a tough one. Parents are overwhelmed with raising children as it is, so how can they take on one more responsibility? ("Ugh! Now I have to be a spiritual teacher, too.") I certainly feel this in my own life as a parent. If spirituality in home life or anywhere else is only a duty or only a responsibility, then it will soon become just one more thing to get done. Yet this is true for congregational programming as well. Ministries can become just one more thing for the congregation to get done. The larger and more critical issue is whether or not home life (in addition to congregational life) can be a powerful source of spiritual meaning for families. If they can, families might find some relief and creative direction in an overwhelming world. Grace, as many people discover, has a way of reordering life around what matters and, by doing so, actually generates energy and passion rather than sapping it.

The large conviction and concern of this book is that faith empowers family life and parenting. Yet to the extent that parents do not feel they are teachers, to the extent that families do not feel they can or know how to practice their faith at home, and to the extent that the expectations on congregations are crushing, then some re-imagination of homes, classrooms, programs, and learning may be in order. I believe a lot of grace is already happening in families and homes, but it is easy to miss. Usually, there is so much pressure for congregational leaders to show they are doing something for families that creating a program is the easiest route. At least we can see it. This is the unintended danger built into "family ministry" and "children's ministry" programs in congregations. In smaller congregations, there may not be enough critical mass or the necessary resources to create new programs or classes. And even in larger congregations, the new program may mean yet one more evening that a parent is away from the kids.

So the issue is as much about imagination and vision as anything else, but that does not make it simple or easy. In fact, it is usually much tougher to stretch our minds and attitudes than it is to create a new program or design a new class. I would like to see home and family life reclaimed as spiritual territory. I would like to see parents recognize themselves as teachers. This does not mean that our children sit in desks and we stand in front of them with a chalkboard giving lectures and handing out grades. (Our images of teaching tend to be captivated by the classroom.) No, our images of teaching and how it happens will be affected by the context. Teaching and learning in the midst of family life have their own character. And they have their own kind of power.

LEARNING AND THE BIBLE

One of the most important resources in the Judeo-Christian tradition for picking up God's rhythms—for religious learning—is the Bible. The scriptures have a way of enlarging our vision, generating creative possibilities, and helping us know what matters. In turn, the Bible can help us pay better attention to the relationship between ourselves and God and discover how deeply meaningful the relationship is. The next two chapters turn to the Bible in order to view family, home, and learning itself against a larger backdrop. As we see our own stories in relation to the story of faith itself, as we see our own families in relation to the family of faith, as we see learning in relation to the source of wisdom itself, all of these become more meaningful to us. This is the ultimate power of learning and the motivation for raising children in faith. Faith helps children perceive themselves more clearly as children of God.

Typically, in religious contexts one of the first questions people ask of any subject, from "family" to "love," is, "What does the Bible say?" Yet the Bible is a big, complex, and intimidating set of texts. (I know many parents feel their sense of inadequacy about spiritual matters most sharply in relation to scripture.) Even those who worship regularly and who read scripture frequently often only get the Bible in fragmented pieces—a reading here, a lesson there; Adam and Eve here, Moses there, Noah, maybe King David or Jesus. But how do these parts relate to each other? That is the challenge. So I turn to the Bible with two hopes. One is to provide a large enough overview of the Bible to help those new to it or intimidated by it to see better how some of its parts relate. The Bible is more than history (it is full of prayers, songs, letters, and teachings), but there is a story being told through it. And knowing that story helps a reader see how individual texts and characters fit within a larger context. If you already know the Bible reasonably well, then you may find the second hope more relevant. The story of faith is deeply relevant to home and family life but not necessarily in obvious ways or on the terms of some of the political debates around "the family." So the next two chapters are a tour, of sorts, through scripture in relation to home. It is not a full-blown Bible study; it is an orientation that attempts to bring out of the background and into the foreground the territory of home and family. For people of faith, this is our family story.

Chapter 2
THE STORY
OF HOME

Our son, David, three years old at the time, was praying at bedtime. He asked God to bless his friends, then his family, pets, and stuffed animals. Finally, he ended the prayer saying, "And God, I miss you."

Huh? I did a mental double take. Did David just say he misses God? Yes, he did. What was that about? What should I do? Part of me wanted to offer him a comforting story or clever advice that would assure him of God's presence, but another part of me was paralyzed by these stark words: "God, I miss you." So instead of saying anything, I kissed him goodnight and went to tell Jane so she could worry, too. Jane was equally puzzled and concerned. The truth is, a parent cannot simply make a three-year-old, or anyone else, feel something they do not, certainly not the presence of God. Whatever we could say or do would fall short of the depth that was generating David's prayer. This was from the heart.

The next morning over our peanut butter and toast, with a touch of fear and trembling, I did bring the matter up with our son. "David, last night when you were praying, you said you missed God."

"Oh yeah," he answered, "but that's okay now."

"What do you mean?"

"Well," he said, "God came to me last night . . . "

I interrupted, "David, you mean like in a dream?" (My modern brain had to find some way to explain this.)

"I dunno, I guess. Anyway, I was playin' in the sandbox behind our old house (we had recently moved across town into an

23

apartment), and God came and said, 'Come, David,' so I followed, and we came here, and now God is here with us in our new home!" He smiled.

David is a teenager now, but that experience still holds power over my imagination. I've quit trying to explain it. Like any deep experience, explaining tends to reduce the fullness of it. I do pay attention to it, however, and when I do, I find, as is true with anything deep, that the experience continues to unfold. I realize how much adults and parents can learn from children, even three-year-olds. I think about the connection between play (in the sandbox) and God. I think about that sandbox itself, which sat on the threshold of our old backyard and the church's backyard—the church where Jane was a pastor. I think about the paradox of praying to a God you miss, who is somehow there and not there at the same time. I ponder the role that rest played—what the Bible might call sabbath. Also striking is how my own eyes were opened at the breakfast table, over the breaking of bread, to the presence of God. And of particular relevance to this book, I consider what a deep connection there can be between a sense of God's presence (or absence) and home.

In one sense, there is a strong tradition of speaking of God as everywhere, that is, as being omnipresent. Yet this is often more talk than a felt assurance. "God is in his heaven and all is right with the world," an old poem goes, which implies that things are best when God is actually somewhere else, resting in glory above this world. Generally, when God is connected to this world, it is often to a religious structure—God's house. It could be a cathedral or temple, a church or synagogue. This connection was evident in my son's experience as well; he could see the church from the sandbox. Then again, in the middle of the night when nobody else was looking, God managed to make it to an apartment as well.

A closer look at the scriptures, however, reveals that this connection between home and God is an old one and persists throughout the Bible. The connection is not necessarily about literal houses or apartments or individual family dwelling places, though these are certainly included. The connection comes through the Bible's attention

THE POWER OF GOD AT HOME

to home as such, to the sense of place—a place to dwell, the places in the hearts of a people. A closer look at the Bible reveals even a *preoccupation* with place—a place for the family of Abraham and Sarah, a place for the human family, a place for the people of Israel, and, finally, even a place for God.

The Bible tells the story of faith. It is part history and genealogy, part poetry and hymns, part wisdom sayings and advice, part politics and law, part geography, part visions, and more. Through it all, God manages to make it into the lives and hearts of humanity. It is too powerful to explain. The Bible tells the story of faith through particular people—the Israelites—and their connection to God and a homeland. The Israelites are descendants of Abraham and Sarah. Just as we cannot understand ourselves fully without knowing our roots, the people of Israel trace their roots back to this ancient couple. But this tracing goes back further yet, to the beginning of life itself and to the first couple, Adam and Eve, whether they are understood symbolically or literally.

In addition to the story of a particular family, the Bible tells a history of a particular place—Canaan—located in the Middle East. In time, this place becomes home to Abraham and Sarah. But to understand the significance of this place, it too must be viewed against a larger backdrop: creation itself. "In the beginning," say the very first words of the Bible, "God created the heavens and the earth." Such was the largest backdrop available to the ancient imagination, and it still can inspire a contemporary heart if we let it.

So while Genesis tells the story of God's relationship with a particular family and a particular place, it also reveals God's relationship to the entire human family and the cosmos itself. The Bible, too, teaches by moving its readers back and forth between parts and wholes. To understand the significance of our own families, the Bible takes us to the family of Abraham and Sarah. No, wait, the picture gets bigger. The Bible takes us to Adam and Eve and the human family. To understand the significance of our own homes, the Bible takes us to Canaan. No, wait, it gets bigger. The Bible takes us to heaven and earth and creation itself.

The Plot

"In the beginning . . ." So the plot begins. These opening words from the first book of scripture, Genesis, start the biblical drama. They let us know that something is about to happen, that a story is about to take place. And like any good drama, the story will have a middle and an end, as well as a beginning. There are many ways of describing and understanding this story, but a very important thread running throughout looks something like the progression shown in the illustration.

This Place–Displacement–Home plot is a basic pattern that repeats itself and gives shape to the Bible in general. I suggest it hesitantly. There is a great danger in suggesting any large theme or plot in the Bible, as schemes like this can make it too easy to reduce the complexities of the material. Some would say there really are no such themes or storylines, as the Bible emerged over centuries and reflects a wide range of concerns. It is really many stories and more. There is certainly truth in this position, but I am interested in simply providing some orientation to the Bible that gives you enough of the sense of a plot that the pieces make a little better sense.

There are differences between Bibles themselves, depending on the translation and the religious tradition. The Jewish community's Bible is what Christians call the Old Testament or Hebrew Bible and is concerned with the origins and ancient history of the people of Israel. Christians extend that history by including the New Testament, which is concerned with Jesus of Nazareth, the origins of Christianity, and the earliest churches. Complicating matters further, the three major branches of Christianity—Eastern Orthodoxy, Roman Catholicism, and Protestantism—hold slightly different versions of the Bible, including some books or verses and not others. Nonetheless, with

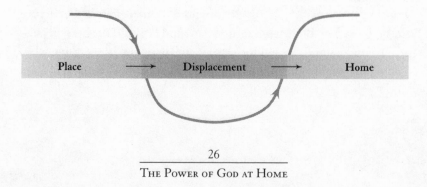

Place   ⟶   Displacement   ⟶   Home

The Power of God at Home

these hesitancies in mind, all these traditions and versions of the Bible share enough in common for our purposes, including this basic storyline of Place–Displacement–Home.

Even so, the storyline is pretty sterile without details: characters, settings, subplots, tensions, and resolutions. Just as *The Wizard of Oz* could be outlined as a story of a girl away from home, the plot only comes to life with the details. So to some of these details we now turn. Over the remainder of this chapter, I illustrate the theme of Place–Displacement–Home in two sections of Israel's history from the Hebrew Bible: (1) Creation–Flood–Canaan and (2) Canaan–Slavery–Kingdom. In the next chapter, I consider three more sections, including the history of Christianity's origins.

CREATION–FLOOD–CANAAN

Creation

"In the beginning when God created the heavens and the earth . . ." The beginning of time in the Bible is also the beginning of place. Physicists have known since Einstein that time and space are intimately connected. Time is tied to space, to place, to the stuff of the universe. There is no story without a setting. And when the Creator looks at this setting, God says, "It is good." In the original Hebrew language, this word *good* means far more than a moral judgment (as in something being good or bad). It is more like a blessing. When God blesses, when God speaks at all in Genesis, it is so. In other words, this place—creation itself—is inherently good. It is fundamentally meaningful, even an expression of God's own nature. God's word creates good space and time. This is the context for human life. This good work of God is humanity's home. *Creation* is the whole that helps us appreciate the goodness of *home*. And the very same power that brings creation into being is key to understanding the power that creates home.

Genesis says that in the beginning the earth was a "formless void," but the Spirit of God (God's *breath* in the Hebrew) fashions from this void, from this empty nothing, creation itself. In the words of John Calvin, "It is the Spirit who, everywhere diffused, sustains all things, causes them to grow, and quickens them in heaven and in earth." From this point of view, God is not simply an Unmoved Mover (as Aristotle put it). Neither is God a cosmic Watchmaker who winds everything up and lets it go (as the eighteenth-century deists put it). Instead, God is the very life of creation. To be sure, God is more than creation, but God's presence continually abides with this world. As the Book of Isaiah tells us, "Holy, holy, holy is the LORD of hosts; the whole earth is full of his glory" (6:3). The picture this paints is a creation gushing with holiness, holding the world together with life. Not just heaven but the whole earth is holy ground. In this biblical cosmology, without God's presence, the universe returns to nothing, to the void. Space and time collapse. If God were only in heaven, all would not be right with the world. If God were to transcend this world completely and exist only in the beyond, as completely "other," this would leave us God-forsaken. And God-forsakenness is not a bad definition of hell.

This intimate relationship between God and the universe not only sets the stage for the biblical family drama but also sets a stage for our own family dramas. From this angle, we can see how earthy the spiritual life actually is. For those of us raising children, who spend a lot of time down low, on the ground even, changing diapers and playing and wiping up spills, the possibility of an earthy spirituality is encouraging. Instead of the lowly world of parenting sinking into a "formless void," in reality it is loaded with creative potential. If holiness has a down-to-earth quality, perhaps our own down-to-earth places are full of possibilities.

This is part of the power of the scriptures; they help us see life in fuller ways, even the most mundane places. The beginning of the Bible, in Genesis, provides the big picture of creation as a powerful backdrop to the significance of the particular place Israel calls home. Likewise, creation, as well as Israel's relation to home, can provide us all with a sense of the sacred possibilities of our own particular homes.

Following the story of creation, Genesis introduces Adam and Eve, the first couple, the mother and father of humanity. Their story starts out great. God provides a place for them—a garden in Eden.

THE POWER OF GOD AT HOME

The garden is full of good things to eat and is pleasant to see as well, says Genesis. It is a land overflowing with life. It is paradise. It is beautiful. It is a place to "be fruitful and multiply." It is home—a home anyone would treasure.

However, Adam and Eve cross a forbidden line. They eat fruit from the one tree they are not supposed to: the tree of knowledge. And all hell breaks loose. Out of fear, they first hide from God's presence (suggesting that fear and God-forsakenness may have a close relationship). But eventually they are caught and cursed. Their punishment is pain for the woman in her own creative act of childbirth and sweat and toil for the man, as he tries to bring life from the soil. For him, the earth shall bring forth only "thorns and thistles."

In addition to this pain and toil, they will return to the dust of the earth, whence they came. Death. A hint of the formless void—nothingness—creeps into the scene. Important to the subject of this book is the fact that Adam and Eve are driven from their place, their home. In stark and disturbing contrast to the scene in the garden abundant with life, we see death. Instead of a paradise dripping with creative power, we see dusty thorns and thistles. Instead of a home where God is heard walking around, Adam and Eve have to go. Adam and Eve embody the first two dimensions of the plot: from Place to Displacement. A Jewish mystical tradition reveals how the loss and pain of displacement not only affects those dislocated but affects God as well. A part of God, in a sense, is also wrenched away from home and wanders with those who suffer homelessness. In this tradition, even God suffers.

Tragically, Adam and Eve do not experience a return to their home. The curse endures for a long time, for generations, beginning with the first children of Adam and Eve. Cain murders his brother Abel. Repeating the theme, Cain too is driven away and is cursed to be a fugitive and a wanderer. The curse continues for many more generations. Genesis continues this story of the cursed degeneration and displacement until it reaches a nadir in the great flood. God is so grieved by humanity, Genesis reports, by human evil, wickedness, and violence, that the Creator is about to become the Destroyer. But not completely. There is a seed of hope: Noah.

Flood

Noah found favor in the LORD's sight, according to the Bible. God is about to re-create, using the household of Noah to do it. Noah's father, Lamech, while naming Noah, says, "Out of the ground that the LORD has cursed this one shall bring us relief from our work and from the toil of our hands." Noah's family represents the seed of life that becomes the hope in the midst of destruction. Reading the story of Noah (see Genesis 5–10) with the earlier chapters in mind reveals important allusions to the original creation story. Water covers the face of the earth (reminiscent of Genesis 1), for example, and God also commands Noah's family to "be fruitful and multiply." In contrast to cursing Adam and Eve, God promises never again to curse the ground or to destroy the earth with a flood. In fact, with the story of Noah, we get the first glimpse of a covenant God makes with the human family that begins reversing the curse generally. Noah, his household, and all kinds of creatures ride out the storm, and new possibilities begin. The household of Noah is fruitful and multiplies, filling the earth with generation after generation, eventually leading to Abram and Sarai, who through encounters with the LORD, become known as Abraham and Sarah.

Again, we can learn not only from the stories directly but from how they are told. The Bible helps us understand a particular household by referring to its roots. We understand Noah better by remembering Adam and Eve as well as Cain and Abel. We understand Abraham and Sarah better through them all. Anything meaningful seems to have this double-sided nature that reaches for the big picture while appreciating the particular details.

Another indirect lesson from scripture comes through the ways in which biblical narratives unfold. Good stories almost always contain a conflict that eventually gets resolved in one way or another. The action in the narrative moves toward righting a situation of wrong. Yet the resolution leads to a deeper appreciation, even a deeper engagement, with one's world. For example, after her misadventures in Oz, Dorothy awakens to a new-found love of her home and friends and family. And in the tragic story of Adam and Eve, the couple's expulsion from their home initiates the conflict that, in turn, moves the larger biblical drama. The power of good stories, when they run deep enough, is that they help us make sense of things and maybe even awaken us to new-found appreciations. They do so by speaking to conditions in life we have to deal with and by sharing sources of hope. Our lives are full of conflicts, losses, new possibilities, and resolutions. This is why family stories are so powerful. Through them, we learn of the challenges our ancestors faced, the losses, the pain, the thorns and thistles in their lives, and how they found sources of hope, strength, and even joy through it all.

Canaan

The story of Abraham and Sarah is no exception. It is full of both promise and conflict. God tells Abram to go to Canaan where he will become "a great nation." God is going to bless Abram and, greater yet, through him "all the families of the earth shall be blessed." The blessing seems to continue the promising atmosphere generated through God's covenant with Noah. This is what promises—deep, genuine promises—do. They shape our lives. As religious education scholar Craig Dykstra suggests, in making promises "people are saying something about their intentions for the future, committing themselves to a particular way of moving through the present into the future." In fact, Dykstra contends that making promises is at the heart of being a family. Sometimes the promises are implied; sometimes they are explicit. I promise to move into the future with you, whether you are my spouse, parent, child, or sibling. I will be there for you.

God promises to be there for Abram and Sarai, to move into the future with them, a great future. And this changes everything (even their names to Abraham and Sarah). But there is a conflict. "Sarai is barren; she had no child," reports Genesis 11. This alone is a conflict against the background of a sparsely populated earth and a command to "be fruitful and multiply." But in relation to the promise, where will this great nation come from? Sarai is barren and old. This is a major conflict. Without offspring, there can be no great nation, no household of blessing to bless all the families of the earth. The LORD, by calling Abram and making promises of land and descendants, actually initiates the story's conflict. And without going into the whole story with its many subplots and false resolutions to the conflict, I will turn to the resolution: a baby. Just as the Creator breathes life into the dust of the earth to form the first human, so life is breathed into the dust of Sarah's womb to create a child, Isaac. For God, time is less a matter of years (Sarah's age) and more a creative act of the Spirit. What a wonderful echo of the original beginning, when the Spirit moved over the formless void (barren womb) bringing life from nothing. So in the land of promise—Canaan—new generations begin taking root. Isaac, in turn, becomes the father of Jacob and Esau. And Jacob, in turn, after his own encounter with God, is renamed Israel. Thus Israel becomes both a people and a place: the great nation promised to Abraham.

The promised land and promised offspring bring resolution to the conflict between becoming a great nation and having no children. But viewed against the larger background of creation, the garden, Adam and Eve, and Noah, we glimpse an even greater resolution. While Adam and Eve are expelled, Abraham and Sarah are called. While Adam and Eve are kicked out, Abraham and Sarah are brought in. While Adam and Eve are cursed, Abraham and Sarah are blessed. The larger impact of the promised land is missed when viewed apart from the larger picture. "Canaan" is loaded with meaning beyond even the powerful story of this one household.

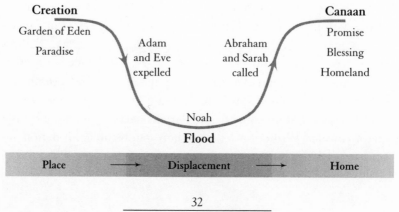

THE POWER OF GOD AT HOME

Christians sometimes have difficulty appreciating the significance of the land of Canaan to the Jewish community, but as one of my colleagues put it, "The land to Jews is like the bread and wine to Christians." Place, here, is all bound up with communion with God. Place is bound up with God's promises; place is bound up with the ancestors and tied to the community of faith. If the Bible focused on this place and this family only in this one story, that would be powerful enough, but the story continues the focus.

CANAAN–SLAVERY–KINGDOM

Canaan

Genesis carries the story of the household of Abraham and Sarah through Isaac and Rebekah, through their son Jacob (Israel) and his wives Rachel and Leah, on to one of their sons, Joseph. The final chapters of Genesis take a troublesome turn. Out of jealousy, Joseph is sold by his own brothers and winds up in quite an adventure in Egypt. He interprets the dreams of the Pharaoh, which predicted a famine, and Egypt is ready when the famine indeed hits the land. The famine reminds the reader again of those cursed thorns and thistles. Yet through Joseph, Egypt is quite prepared. Searching for food, Jacob's household (brothers and all) winds up in Egypt, too, where they reunite and reconcile with Joseph. The promised descendants of Abraham and Sarah are left in Egypt, well fed, as the Book of Genesis closes. Although the story of Joseph, with all its marvelous twists and turns and conflicts and reconciliations and resolutions, seems like a happy ending, we get a clue that all's well only for the moment. Egypt should only be a temporary situation—a place to wait out the famine. The last three verses of Genesis are revealing.

> Then Joseph said to his brothers, "I am about to die; but God will surely come to you, and bring you up out of this land to the land that he swore to Abraham, to Isaac, and to Jacob." So Joseph made the Israelites swear, saying, "When God comes to you, you shall carry up my bones from here." And

Joseph died, being one hundred ten years old; he was embalmed and placed in a coffin in Egypt [50:24–26].

Genesis reminds the reader here that home is the land sworn to the ancestors. Home is not Egypt. Jacob's household in Egypt introduces a new conflict. The Israelites in Egypt are something like Adam and Eve's exile from the garden. The famine not only echoes the curse of working the ground only to get thistles and thorns but it echoes dry wombs as well and the dry dust of the earth apart from the moist breath of life. To peoples surrounded by desert, these must have been powerful images. Being embalmed and placed in a coffin in Egypt is an ominous ending to Genesis—one that reminds the reader of the larger dilemma of being cut off from home. And the ending foreshadows the monumental conflict that comes next: a titanic confrontation between Egypt's Pharaoh and Israel's God, with life-and-death stakes.

Slavery

As the next book of the Bible—Exodus—begins, we learn that Joseph's household is indeed fruitful and multiplies. However, in time a king arises in Egypt "who knew not Joseph." Out of fear of these descendants of Jacob (Israel), the Pharaoh treats them ruthlessly. He turns them into slaves and eventually even orders the deaths of all their newborn males. Death, slavery, and oppression abound in this foreign land, in this land where Joseph is embalmed, in this land that is not home. Displacement made the Israelites vulnerable, and the Pharaoh took advantage of the situation.

In Genesis, as the story is about to reach its lowest point with the flood, a seed of hope emerges in the figure of Noah. Noah bridges the old world before the flood with a new humanity afterward. In Exodus, the story reaches a low point in the history of Israel's household; it reaches to slavery and oppression. But God hears the people's cries and raises a new figure of hope in Moses. Moses becomes a bridge between the old world in Egypt and new possibilities in the promised land. While the Book of Exodus charts Israel's escape from slavery, the next three books of the Bible—Leviticus, Numbers, and Deuteronomy—describe the events between the Israelites' liberation from Egypt and their new life in that land flowing with milk and honey, the land sworn to Abraham, Isaac, and Jacob. It was not an easy journey.

Much contemporary imagery for the spiritual life can be traced to this generations-long travel through the desert by the Israelites. The religious life is frequently described as a journey or a pilgrimage or a walk. Some even speak of faith as stages along a journey. One of my favorite images comes from the old Appalachian hymn, "I Wonder as I Wander." These are important images, and they certainly capture dimensions of the spiritual life, but left to themselves they are incomplete. As theologian and historian Wendy Wright points out, these images often reflect the experience of those who may have literally gone into the wilderness on spiritual journeys by themselves (unlike the Israelites), those not bound to caring for families. In contrast to such an emphasis on moving and wandering, Wright suggests we also need language that appreciates the spiritual possibilities of "dwelling." This insight is true to the biblical story at this point. Ultimately, dwelling was the hope of the Israelites' spiritual journey through the desert. So although wandering is sometimes a reality of life, wandering is not the point of life.

The Israelites' journey to the homeland was indeed a wandering, indirect one, lasting years and years. There is a story to this, too. Biblically, the wandering life is described as a consequence of not following the LORD whole-heartedly (Numbers 32:13). The Israelites got near the promised land early on, but they were afraid to enter, and they wanted to return to Egypt. God in turn curses this generation to a life of wandering (Numbers 14). Wandering, here, has overtones of Adam and Eve's expulsion and Cain's punishment for murdering his brother. Wandering is a curse. Wandering is homelessness. Wandering is something to be relieved of. Dwelling is relief.

So, as the story of the Israelites continues in the Bible, the promised land of dwelling accumulates even more layers of meaning. The promised land is relief from wandering, escape from Egypt's slavery, the land sworn to the ancestors, and the great nation pledged to Abraham. Symbolically, the land is even connected back to Adam and Eve's expulsion. The promised land represents the garden, fertility, life, and even creation itself. It is home. It is spiritual home and material home as well. Part of the Bible's power is that it reveals the spiritual possibilities in the material world. In fact, the distinction itself, between spiritual and material, is not very biblical. Creation, places, homes—even our own apartments and houses— when viewed in this large perspective that the scriptures offer, take on deep layers of meaning.

In the Book of Deuteronomy, the fifth book of the Bible and the last book of the part of the Bible called *Torah* (Hebrew for "the Law"), the story takes place on the threshold of Israel's return to home after a generation of wandering. Before the Israelites cross the Jordan to enter the land, Moses addresses the people. In the process, Deuteronomy illustrates the biblical intertwining of place and time, of home and the generations, and God. Deuteronomy 5 reiterates the commandments, but Deuteronomy 6:4 (called the *shema*, which is Hebrew for "listen" or "hear") summarizes and urges the very meaning of the commandments, "Hear, O Israel: The LORD is our God, the LORD alone." Moses continues:

> You shall love the LORD your God with all your heart, and with all your soul, and with all your might. Keep these words that I am commanding you today in your heart. Recite them to your children and talk about them when you are at home and when you are away, when you lie down and when you rise. Bind them as a sign on your hand, fix them as an emblem on your forehead, and write them on the doorposts of your house and on your gates [6:5–9].

Keeping these words, loving God with all we are, and teaching the children are all part of the same fabric. They go together. They work together. The importance of remembering God in the promised land is emphasized. And the importance of remembering God in our homes is underscored.

Why? What is Moses worried about? Deuteronomy reveals the worry that the people would forget it was the LORD who brought them out of Egypt and to this land flowing with milk and honey. Not only would there be tempting foreign gods as they entered the land but time itself—the passing of the generations—would make it easy to forget what God has done. It would be easy to forget the holy source of their liberation and land. Deuteronomy predicts that children will eventually ask, "What is the meaning of the decrees and the statutes and the ordinances that the LORD our God has commanded you?" (6:20). Children do ask tough questions: Why do we do this? Why do we do that? Why do we worship? Why do we pray? What good is it all? Children, like adults, inevitably begin asking questions of meaning; they too want to know more than how-to.

Deuteronomy sees it coming. A generation or more removed from the events of Egypt or settling in the land, the next generation may not appreciate the practices of their elders without knowing the convictions and stories to undergird them. They might not appreciate this God—there are many gods from which to choose—without understanding the connection to the ancestors, freedom, and the land. Therefore, Deuteronomy advises: talk to your children; let them know what's happened—the hard times and the good; tell them the story. "Say to your children, 'We were Pharaoh's slaves in Egypt, but the LORD brought us out of Egypt with a mighty hand. He brought us out from there in order to bring us in, to give us the land that he promised on oath to our ancestors'" (6:20–23).

The Book of Deuteronomy makes it very clear that knowing the LORD alone is God, that teaching the children, that remembering the ancestors, that the land, and that liberation are all bound together to form a faithful whole. They are our roots. Put negatively, worshiping other gods, not hearing our children, not teaching the children, forgetting the ancestors, slavery, and rootlessness form a destructive pattern. They are the danger. And Moses makes the dangers quite clear as the Israelites are about to cross the Jordan to home. Moses addresses these stakes while standing on the threshold between the desert and the promised land. It is a threshold between wandering and dwelling. And such a threshold reveals the stakes involved in whether or not we teach our children. Teaching and learning in communities of faith, whether in families or in congregations, is an extension of the *shema,* of remembering the Lord is God and living it out.

Kingdom

In reviewing the events from Exodus to the promised land, we see that the plot is repeating. But along the way it gathers new layers of meaning. The books following Deuteronomy—Joshua through Kings—tell the story of the Israelites in the promised land after their freedom from Egypt. First, the books of Joshua and Judges chart out the initial stages of establishing this land as a nation: crossing the Jordan, fighting battles with other peoples, and attempting to rule through judges. Then the books of Samuel and Kings describe the establishment of Israel as a nation "like other nations," that is, with a king. Saul is anointed king, followed by King David, followed by David's son Solomon.

It is under Solomon (approximately 1000 B.C.E.) that the first temple of the LORD is built in Jerusalem. This is a crucial moment in the history of Israel. This temple is built on a promise and condition:

> Now the word of the LORD came to Solomon, "Concerning this house that you are building, if you will walk in my statutes, obey my ordinances, and keep all my commandments by walking in them, then I will establish my promise with you, which I made to your father David. I will dwell among the children of Israel, and will not forsake my people Israel" [1 Kings 6:11–13].

This house, this temple, becomes the center of worship and a powerful expression of God dwelling among the people. It raises again the tension between God being everywhere and God being in a particular place. But as rabbi and scholar Abraham Heschel suggests, "Even those who believe that God is everywhere set aside a place for a sanctuary. For the sacred to be sensed at all moments everywhere, it must also at this moment be somewhere." The temple sanctifies dwelling. The people of God are finally home, just as God

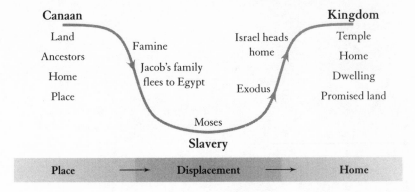

Canaan   Kingdom

Land   Famine   Israel heads home   Temple

Ancestors   Home

Home   Jacob's family flees to Egypt   Exodus   Dwelling

Place   Promised land

Moses

Slavery

Place   ⟶   Displacement   ⟶   Home

is at home dwelling among the children of Israel. The conflict initiated in Eden is resolved. God and humanity again can live together.

⋆✦⋆ ⋆✦⋆ ⋆✦⋆

Like the watercolorist who layers wash of transparent paint upon wash upon wash, color explodes with beauty. So it is with the promised land for Israel; dwelling explodes with meaning. Place, land, home, dwelling, the temple, and the presence of God are all layers of a sacred picture. If this is so for the land, for Israel's spiritual, material home, then maybe something analogous can happen for all our particular dwelling places. Maybe our own homes, our own places mean more when we understand them in relation to this bigger picture.

Perhaps, as Wendy Wright suggests, we can appreciate the spiritual life as dwelling as much as it can also be a journey. Certainly, raising children is a journey, but they don't need us running off being spiritual everywhere else. Children need our presence; they need a meaningful somewhere.

Chapter 3

AT HOME AMONG MORTALS

The story of faith is the story of life: families and homes, blessing and curse, conflict, loss, hope, love, and more. In the scriptures, faith and life are so intertwined that a reader would be hard pressed to know where one begins and the other ends. Our ancestors in faith could sense God's presence in the titanic confrontations with a Pharaoh, as well as in the simplest deeds and prayers of a child. To them, the temple and the doorposts of our homes alike were crucial to remembering God. As the Israelites built homes and the temple, as they established themselves as a nation like other nations, they reach a high point in their history. But the story of faith reveals that, as is true in all of life, high points are difficult to sustain.

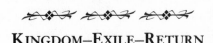

KINGDOM–EXILE–RETURN

Kingdom

The kingdom under David holds a grand position in biblical history. The biblical history of the kings generally, especially when the prophets are included, is often confusing and intimidating to readers of the Bible, both new readers and seasoned. But it is essential to the faith story, especially as the history reveals the passion of God for love and justice. David, who slew Goliath as a boy, grows up to be a great ruler, according to the scriptures. Even so, through the brilliant honesty of the Hebrew scriptures, David is remembered as a grand-yet-flawed character. Not only did he have an affair with another man's wife, Bathsheba, but he set her husband, Uriah, up to be killed in battle. No soap opera or tabloid could portray a more wicked plot. It takes the prophet Nathan to expose this abuse of the king's power to David himself, and the LORD promises trouble for David's house. In the Bible, trouble in the king's house is trouble for the kingdom itself. David's injustice sows seeds of trouble that do not fully bloom for a generation or two.

Solomon, son of David and Bathsheba, continues the greatness of the monarchy for many years. His wisdom is still celebrated, and under his reign a temple is constructed—a center of worship. But worship also gets Solomon in trouble, according to the Book of Kings. Solomon worships foreign gods. What Moses worried about (not remembering that the LORD is God alone) occurs. Just as Solomon's sacred loyalties divide, idolatry divides the great nation.

> Therefore the LORD said to Solomon, "Since this has been your mind and you have not kept my covenant and my statutes that I have commanded you, I will surely tear the kingdom from you and give it to your servant. Yet for the sake of your father David I will not do it in your lifetime; I will tear it out of the hand of your son" [1 Kings 11:11–12].

Again, trouble with the king is tantamount to trouble with the nation. Two of Solomon's sons fight over who should be the next king; like most greed-based struggles for power, this one leads to conflict and tragedy. The tribes of Israel split into two kingdoms, one in the north and one in the south. The kingdom in the north made Samaria the capital and took the name *Israel.* The kingdom in the south kept Jerusalem as its capital and took the name *Judah,* from King David's tribe. This split degenerates further into many abuses of power within both nations. Time and again, the scriptures report of rulers in this era who "do not walk in the ways of the LORD."

During this period, most of the prophets in the Bible emerge. Several whole books of the Bible are devoted to the message and vision of the prophets, but appreciating these is difficult without understanding their general historical context. Yet, as we appreciate the context, I believe the prophets become an even greater force to reckon with, and their message and vision take on even greater relevance for life with children, especially the most vulnerable children. How so?

Often we think of prophets as those odd people who can predict the future. But in the Bible, the predictions of a prophet are more of an extension of a deeper message than some kind of demonstration of magic or clairvoyance. The message of a biblical prophet is clear: God will not tolerate the abuse of power. Such abuse, especially with those holding a lot of power, will breed trouble. For example, Amos rails against injustice and warns the people: "Seek the LORD and live, or he will break out against the house of Joseph like fire, and it will devour Bethel, with no one to quench it. Ah, you that turn justice to wormwood, and bring righteousness to the ground!" (Amos 5:6–7).

Many of us who tend to emphasize the love of God get uncomfortable with the vision of such an angry God. Yet what is God angry about? Ways of treating others that betray love and care. "Therefore because you trample on the poor and take from them levies of grain, you have built houses of hewn stone, but you shall not live in them; you have planted pleasant vineyards, but you shall not drink their wine" (Amos 5:11).

Injustice does not go unnoticed, according to Amos; it will be cursed. And the curse itself is the undoing of the precious gift of land and home. Forgetting the Holy One's passion for justice and love leads to the loss of home, according to the prophets. A reader must be careful here not to reverse the logic. If people are homeless, whether a man on the street, a family left homeless by poverty, or the Israelites in Egypt, it does not follow that God is punishing those people. Such logic would inflame the prophet even more because it rationalizes injustice.

Injustice—trampling the poor, taking advantage of others, misusing one's power—will lead to conflict and strife in the nation. The Bible foreshadows the trouble to come to the land in the troublesome story of King David, Bathsheba, and Uriah. Again, the well-being or trouble of a king's household in these ancient times reveals the well-being or trouble of the nation. The Bible also reveals the role of the prophet in the same story. It is the prophet Nathan who tells David about a rich man who took a poor man's lamb. David is outraged and says the man deserves to die. Nathan reveals, "You are the man!" (2 Samuel 12).

In the name of the LORD, the prophet exposes evil. This prophetic dimension of the biblical story reveals a prophetic dimension to faith itself—a dimension that becomes particularly important when we look at sin and evil in the chapters ahead. Children in our own households, in our nation, and in our world are so often in the most vulnerable position in relation to the use and abuse of power. And for now, through the biblical prophets, we can see that faith has something to say about this.

Exile

Though there are a few exceptions among the kings (for example, Josiah), conflict and decline spread among these two kingdoms until the northern kingdom of Israel finally falls to the neighboring nation of Assyria (722 B.C.E.) and is annexed by it. Later the southern kingdom collapses, as Jerusalem surrenders to Babylon's Nebuchadnezzar (586 B.C.E.). As Jerusalem falls, some people flee to Egypt; many are captured and deported to Babylon to live in exile. The city is ransacked; the temple in Jerusalem—the place of God's dwelling—is burned. Like Adam and Eve, the children of God are expelled from their home. There is a loss of paradise, a loss of the land flowing with milk and honey. The agony of this is expressed in Psalm 137:

> By the rivers of Babylon—there we sat down and there we wept when we remembered Zion. On the willows there we hung up our harps. For there our captors asked us for songs, and our tormentors asked for mirth, saying, "Sing us one of the songs of Zion!" How could we sing the Lord's song in a foreign land? [1–4].

Out of the depths of this despair, this national homelessness, the people in exile long for a sign of hope. They long for a savior who can, like Moses, once again lead the children of Jacob back to the land sworn to the ancestors. They yearn for a new day, like the old day, with a kingdom like the one under David, a righteous leader. At this low point in the history of the Israelites, the prophets play another kind of role. As long as injustice flourishes, the prophets foresee disaster, but once disaster does strike, the prophets become the very ones to express hope—hope for a new day, a day of return to the LORD and the land. "For I am about to create new heavens and a new earth," proclaims Isaiah in the name of God. "I am about to create Jerusalem as a joy. I will rejoice in Jerusalem and delight in my people; no more shall the sound of weeping be heard in it or the cry of distress. They shall build houses and inhabit them" (Isaiah 65).

These low moments in the history of Israel make clear a paradox about God. Although God is deeply connected to the promised land—to dwelling there—and to homes and to the temple, God is not limited to the land, homes, or the temple. To those displaced, this is good news, given that the temple has gone down in flames. There is still hope. The LORD is the Creator and God of the entire universe—the heavens and the earth. God is greater than the Pharaoh, greater than Babylon's king. Again, God is somewhere particularly; God is everywhere. This tense affirmation is important theologically because it helps distinguish God from the idols, the false gods. Idols are gods that are too small to handle life. Idols are narrowed to their own little worlds and tend to narrow the world of their worshipers. Idols can be statues of gods, or they can be drugs or even ideas. But they are human constructions that promise salvation and yet never fully deliver. When times get rough or the world proves complicated, idols collapse and return to the dust whence they came. Idols are hopeless. There is nothing more to them. Instead, hope springs from sensing that the One who created the universe, who created humanity from the dust of the earth, still creates and can again breathe life into the barren deserts of hopelessness.

On the other side of this paradox, a god who is incapable of connecting to a particular people, to a particular place, or to a particular temple—a god who is just vaguely everywhere—is not very hopeful either. Such a disconnected god would not care, would be apathetic about injustice or oppression. Without particular connections, there is no love. Such a god is hopeless.

To reiterate the paradox, Israel worships a God who is both everywhere and somewhere, larger than the universe and in love with it at the same time. In this Holy One rests hope. Not only is this insight important during our own times of struggle, in our own places of exile, it is critical to the spiritual lives of our children. Children need particular connections to love in their lives—families and homes, friends and congregations. But they also need to learn the ways in which God can be present in the larger world—in communities, in creation, in foreign nations, in strangers even. This is tricky because our children are especially vulnerable, as the prophets might point out, to the abuse of power, both in our own homes and congregations and among strangers. So parents are in a tough position negotiating this territory. But that is all the more reason we need the wisdom and guidance of our ancestors in faith. We need a continued word from the prophets to keep us watching out for the vulnerable, and we need their promise of hope in the midst of hard times.

Return

One of the most powerful expressions of hope in this period of exile comes through the Book of Ezekiel. The prophet Ezekiel has a vision of the valley of dry bones. The people in exile are as lifeless as dried-out skeletons. Yet, as the vision continues, God says, "I am going to open your graves, and bring you up from your graves, O my people; and I will bring you back to the land of Israel" (37:12).

Home, here, promises new life. And reminiscent of Genesis, the vision portrays God breathing life into dry bones, resurrecting life from death. The Book of Ezekiel goes on to offer several more visions of hope. For example, in the twenty-fifth year of exile, God shows Ezekiel a vision of a temple, promising to give the land back to the people of Israel. It takes several chapters to detail this temple—a kind of blueprint not only for the reconstruction of the building but for the reconstruction of hope itself. This vision culminates with the river of life flowing from the temple. "Wherever the river goes, every living creature that swarms will live, and there will be very many fish, once these waters reach there. It will become fresh; and everything will live where the river goes" (Ezekiel 47:9).

The vision goes on to describe people spreading their nets for all kinds of fish, and growing on the banks of the river are all kinds of trees for food. "Their leaves will not wither nor their fruit fail, but they will bear fresh fruit every month, because the water for them flows from the sanctuary. Their fruit will be for food, and their leaves for healing" (47:12).

This vision bears out the deep connection between the temple, the land, lush paradise, and creative power. Once again, God plants a seed of hope that leads to new life. And as did Noah and Moses, a person bridges the old situation with the new. But the unlikely figure of a hopeful new start, for a return to Jerusalem, was a foreign king—King Cyrus of Persia. This underscores the point that the LORD is not bound only to one place or one people but still cares about these people and this place. Persia, under Cyrus, defeats the captors—Babylon (539 B.C.E.)—and Cyrus issues an edict: "Thus says King Cyrus of Persia: The LORD, the God of heaven, has given me all the kingdoms of the earth, and he has charged me to build him a house at

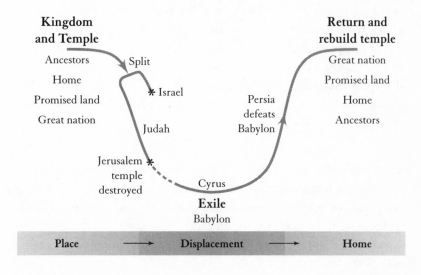

Jerusalem, which is in Judah. Whoever is among you of all his people, may the LORD his God be with him! Let him go up" (2 Chronicles 36:23). The books of Ezra and Nehemiah next describe the return of the people to Judah and the rebuilding of Jerusalem, including the temple. Finally, Israel is home.

The story of Israel is certainly more complex than presented here. Many of the biblical books have not been mentioned, that is, several of the prophetic books, as well as those sometimes classified as "the Writings" or so-called wisdom material such as Job, Ecclesiastes, or Proverbs. These wisdom materials, particularly, can stand alone from the history more easily than other books and still be appreciated, but only to a degree. It is still helpful to know how the Book of Job, for example, relates to the history of Israel. Job is the story of a good man who loses everything. He wrestles with the most profound questions life presents: the loss of family and health, with suffering and evil, with justice and redemption. Most scholars believe Job was probably written during the Babylonian exile (around the sixth century, B.C.E.). So on the one hand, Job could be the archetypal righteous person who suffers undeservedly; on the other, Job could represent the people of Israel in exile. The plot of Job reflects the history of Israel. He enjoys a good home, then suffers intense loss and destruction (a kind of displacement), then home and family are re-created. Again, the plot alone, whether in the Book of Job or the history of Israel, does not communicate the depth and power of the story. That comes through the details, through careful reading and reflection, and through a lifetime of learning.

The story of Jesus and Christianity is next. But the Christian church, centuries ago, made it clear that Christians cannot understand their story without understanding its roots in Israel. And once again home is important, though in a slightly different way. This time the descendants of Abraham and Sarah still live in the homeland, but it is occupied.

THE POWER OF GOD AT HOME

JESUS–CRUCIFIXION–RESURRECTION

Jesus

Though not quite as obvious, the plot of Place–Displacement–Home is reflected in at least a couple of ways in the Christian New Testament. Seeing this plot in the history of Israel helps readers appreciate the larger whole of which Christianity is a part. In one way, the plot occurs through the historical circumstances of the early church, and in another it happens in the very life and death of Jesus of Nazareth.

As the New Testament tells the story of Jesus and the earliest churches and Christians, it does so at a time when the promised land is overtaken by the Romans. This was a different kind of exile. A modern analogy might be France or the Netherlands occupied by the Nazis during World War II. In relation to the plot of Place–Displacement–Home, the displacement here is a displacement of power. In other words, the land alone does not guarantee a sense of home. If security and freedom are missing, the place is just not home. The Roman army made home miserable. And once again the people of God longed for a leader, an anointed one (in Hebrew, *messiah*), who could rule with integrity, justice, and righteousness. For Christians, Jesus of Nazareth was this messiah and more. Christians believe that in this human one, the presence of God dwelled fully. In many ways, to Christians the life of Jesus was like the temple of God, where God meets and dwells with humanity.

The New Testament tells the stories of Jesus' life, ministry, death, resurrection, and more. Specifically, the first four books—the gospels of Matthew, Mark, Luke, and John—tell the story of Jesus himself. The remaining books tell about the followers of Jesus, the early churches, and the persecution and conflicts that emerged in early Christianity. The New Testament then ends with the Book of Revelation and its vision of God's coming.

Jesus himself was Jewish, and Christianity was a movement within Judaism, but it spreads well beyond it. As the Apostle Paul puts it in the Book of Romans, with Jesus Christ those who were outside the family of Abraham, those called gentiles, are "grafted" in (Romans 11). Through Jesus, even gentiles enter the family of faith. The blessings of the God of Israel pour out as a hope and salvation to the whole world. God adopts households, including but beyond Abraham's, reminding us of the original covenant where "all the families of the earth shall be blessed" (Genesis 12:3). Once again, as Moses discovered and Ezekiel saw, in the midst of a displacement God's power is not confined to one place or even to the temple. The blessings of God are for all the families of the earth.

This spirit of adoption infuses the words of Jesus himself when he says, "'Who is my mother, and who are my brothers?' And pointing to his disciples, he says, 'Here are my mother and my brothers! For whoever does the will of my Father in heaven is my brother and sister and mother'" (Matthew 12:48–50). Sometimes this statement is taken to mean that Jesus is against families. But as family ministry scholar Diana Garland points out, a second look at the passage reveals that "Jesus was not denying his relationship with his mother and brothers; he was *widening the circle*." For Garland, adoption and covenant are at the core of a biblical understanding of family. In other words, the ability to graft in outsiders is at the heart of what it means to be a family. Marriage itself illustrates this point. To marry is to open yourself to another, originally an outsider, in the most intimate and personal ways. Your very identity changes. You open yourself not only to your partner but to his or her family as well, and vice versa. In marriages that value mutuality in the relationship, each partner is grafting in the life of another while being grafted into the life of the other. Parenting does the same. Children, whether by birth or adoption, have to be grafted into the family. At the same time, children change the identity of a family. So Jesus points to the very heart of family life, to our capacity to be open to and love others. And he stretches the meaning of family.

The theological significance of widening the circle of family is not new with the New Testament. The Book of Ruth in the Hebrew scriptures, for example, powerfully illustrates the significance of the openness, love, and commitment born of deep relationships. Ruth herself is a Moabite woman, an outsider, who married into an Israelite

THE POWER OF GOD AT HOME

family. Though a foreigner to Israel's household, she remains devoted to her mother-in-law Naomi, even after Ruth's Israelite husband dies. She does so by choice. Ruth says to Naomi, "Do not press me to leave you or to turn back from following you! Where you go, I will go; where you lodge, I will lodge; your people shall be my people, and your God my God" (Ruth 1:16). Ruth stays with Naomi and, in the process, winds up being the grandmother of King David himself— no small place in the history of Israel. So we can notice the role that grafting plays in both Israel and Christianity.

Crucifixion

We appreciate the ministry of Jesus better if we appreciate the oppressive context of the Roman occupation and the hunger, disease, injustice, and slavery that went with it. Jesus engaged in a ministry of teaching, accompanied by feeding, healing, forgiving, and liberating. All of these served to empower people displaced from power. These acts were signs that God was indeed at work, even in the midst of the terrible occupation. There are differences to be sure, but there are parallels between Jesus and Noah, Moses, and even Cyrus. Jesus is part of a long creative history in which God brings about hope and salvation. Feeding, healing, and liberation of all kinds were signs of the kingdom of God, of God's hand at work, mightier than the current regime.

Although Jesus' ministry was a seed of hope to the hopeless, it was a threat to the powers of occupation. So they stopped him. And the only thing worse than having no hope is having received a glimpse of hope and then losing it. His followers were devastated. When Jesus was arrested and killed, the people's dreams of a leader who would remove the Romans were shattered. As Cleopas, a follower of Jesus, put it, "We had hoped that he was the one to redeem Israel" (Luke 24:21). The crucifixion, the death of Jesus on a cross as a criminal, becomes the ultimate loss for those who hoped. This execution embodied the power of Rome. This death embodied the broken spirit of a people who had hoped for liberation. Rome held the power of life and death itself. Where was God?

If the story had ended with death, it may never have been told. But the story does not end there. As the gospel according to Luke puts it, two of the followers of Jesus were walking along a road, away from Jerusalem, when Jesus joined them, but they did not recognize him since he had been killed. He interpreted the scriptures to them, explaining how the Messiah must suffer. They still did not recognize him until "he was at the table with them, he took bread, blessed and broke it, and gave it to them. Then their eyes were opened, and they recognized him; and he vanished from their sight" (Luke 24:30–31). They returned to Jerusalem—the place of the temple, the city of king David, the place of the crucifixion—where they discovered that Jesus had appeared to other disciples as well.

Resurrection

Each of the gospels tells of the resurrection in its own way, but they all testify to the risen presence of the one who had been killed. Biblical scholars, historians, and Christians themselves debate over how to explain this, how literally or symbolically to take the accounts, but the overriding sense in either case is that the early followers of Jesus discovered that the one who had been crucified was now alive. Implied is the fact that, ultimately, the Romans were not the power of life and death any more than the Pharaoh had been. As the prophet Ezekiel once proclaimed, even dry bones can live again; even graves cannot hold back the breath of life. God is present even in the midst of death, raising new possibilities for love, life, and freedom.

The followers of Jesus recognized and celebrated this life and power in the bread and in the wine—the body broken, the blood poured out. To this day, the bread and wine are loaded with the power of life.

But even this bread and the wine hearken back to the Jewish Passover meal with its bread and wine. The Passover meal remembers the Exodus from Egypt. It is a meal that remembers God's creative power over the royal power of the Pharaoh. This meal celebrates freedom from slavery and the security to dwell in a land sworn to the ancestors. In the promised land people can harvest their own grain for bread, they can plant vineyards to make their own wine. When Jews celebrate the Passover in their homes every year, they are remembering God's power for freedom, for security, for dwelling, and more. When Christians celebrate communion, they are building upon a long history of God's presence, God's freedom, and God's life-giving power. Rabbi Nancy Fuchs, in her beautiful book *Our Share of Night, Our Share of Morning,* which explores spirituality and parenting, tells the story of a young girl who remembers how she and her grandmother every year would bake a special bread for Easter.

> On Good Friday afternoon, in a solemn mood, they knead the dough. Then they place the bread in the oven, and grandmother and granddaughter sit sadly together, thinking about the crucifixion of Christ. Soon, however, the wonderful aroma of baking bread begins to penetrate the gloom, and their mood lightens. On Sunday morning, the grandmother hands her granddaughter a piece of the bread. As she tastes it, the girl knows in her very bones that "Christ has risen."

The story connects the deep meaning of Easter with the meaningful relationship between a grandmother and granddaughter. When such connections happen, even the smell of baking bread can take on new life and power.

The story of Jesus reflects, in so many ways, the history of Israel. The cross and Christ's suffering embody the suffering of the Israelites in Egypt, in Babylon, and in the Roman occupation. The resurrection reflects the new life that God creates in the midst of death and suffering: returning to the promised land, building the new temple, raising dry bones. For Christians who believe in Jesus as the Son of God, God is meeting death directly, revealing a paradoxical kind of power. God is not wielding the sword of death to battle death. Jesus is not a warrior savior. Instead, through Jesus Christ, God meets the hell of God-forsakenness with presence, with dwelling. As the Apostles' Creed of the early church puts it, the Son of God "descended into hell, and on the third day he rose from the dead." God takes on death, meeting it with eternal life. The Book of 1 Corinthians puts it this way: "For since death came through a human being, the resurrection of the dead has also come through a human being; for as all die in Adam, so all will be made alive in Christ" (15:21–22). The author, the Apostle Paul, is reaching as far back in biblical history as he possibly can to interpret the significance and scope of this resurrection.

The result is an outpouring of life, an outpouring of the Spirit of life, among the early Christian communities. As the Book of Acts describes, the Spirit of God that raised Christ was the same Spirit raising new communities of hope, even in the midst of the Roman occupation. Jesus, like the temple, embodies God's dwelling.

Christians rehearse this connection between destruction and creation, between death and life, with baptism. In baptism, we die with Christ and we are raised to new life with Christ. In traditions that baptize infants, parents are placing their children in the context of this kind of power—the power of life. Scholar and priest John Westerhoff tells of a baptism he witnessed in a small church in Latin America. "The congregation began the mournful sounds of a funeral hymn as a solemn procession moved down the aisle. A father carried a child's coffin he had made from wood; a mother carried a bucket of water from the family well."

Water is poured into the coffin; the baby's skin is covered with embalming oil. The priest lowers the baby into the coffin and water exclaiming, "I kill you in the name of the Father and of the Son and of the Holy Spirit." The congregation and parents shout, "Amen,"

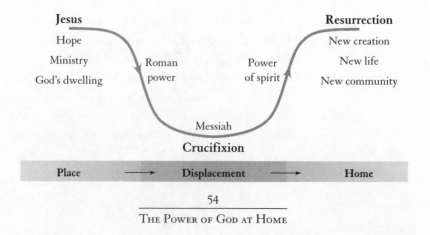

THE POWER OF GOD AT HOME

then the priest lifts the child and declares, "And I resurrect you that you might love and serve the Lord."

The congregation, as he tells it, "then broke into a joyous Easter hymn."

TEMPLE–DESTRUCTION–NEW CREATION

In one sense, the life, death, and resurrection of Jesus (and therefore baptism as well) embody the plot in the history of Israel. But there is another echo of it in the New Testament, more directly connected to the temple, to Jerusalem, and to the promise of God's dwelling.

Temple–Destruction

At the very time when the first churches were forming, when much of the New Testament was being written down (during the middle to latter part of the first century), Jerusalem was once again falling apart at the hands of a foreign army. Once again, the people of Israel were being persecuted. Finally, in the year 69, the temple itself was destroyed. Many early Christians saw a close relationship between the destruction of the temple and the destruction of the Messiah. In the second chapter of the gospel of John, Jesus says, "Destroy this temple, and in three days I will raise it up." Those who heard him pointed out that the rebuilding of the temple had been going on for forty-six years. How was he going to raise it in three days? "But," as John continues, "he was speaking of the temple of his body. After he was raised from the dead, his disciples remembered that he had said this; and they believed the scripture and the word that Jesus had spoken" (19–22).

So layers of meaning build. The temple is the heart of the promised land; it is the "somewhere" of God's dwelling; it is the power of home; how painful its destruction must have been. And early Christian communities saw a parallel between the destruction of the temple and the crucifixion of Jesus. Layers of loss and sorrow build.

In my own history, about a decade ago, the church in which I was raised burned completely out. Here was the building where I was baptized, confirmed, and married; it was where I worshiped, learned, and celebrated God's presence. This was my first temple, and here it was reduced to char and rubble. As my parents watched it burned, their pain was compounded by knowing that all three of their children had such history loaded into this place, this building. For the Jews, the second destruction of the Jerusalem temple was an experience compounded by centuries of history, centuries of ancestors, generations of worship and learning and celebrating God's presence. To this day, the Wailing Wall of Jerusalem—all that remains of that temple—is a powerful testimony to the significance of the temple, of history, of the generations, of the land, of place, of a homeland.

The first century was a devastating time for Jews and Christians alike, apocalyptic times even. The world as they knew it was crumbling, and persecution and suffering were everywhere. Such conflict has a way of breeding more conflict, even among friends, small communities, religious groups, and families. Political conflict and persecution from on high (the Romans) can replicate itself in all kinds of ways, and much of the New Testament, written during these times, reveals such conflict and suffering. So even though Christians believed that the Messiah, a Deliverer, a Savior, had indeed come, there was still a sense in which God's kingdom had not come in full. Though believers experienced an outpouring of the Spirit, the indwelling presence of God, it was only a partial glimpse. As the Apostle Paul put it in 1 Corinthians 13:12, "For now we see in a mirror, dimly, but then we will see face to face." The "then" refers to a time yet to come. In another place, Paul interprets the events around Christ in agricultural imagery. The raising of Christ from the dead represents the "first fruits" of what is to come. "But in fact Christ has been raised from the dead, the first fruits of those who have died" (1 Corinthians 15:20).

As Paul interprets the significance of Jesus, he develops yet another layer of meaning to the story of faith. The land sworn to the ancestors—land now occupied by rulers, authorities, and enemies of God—has become a place of death. Death, occupation, principalities and powers, and persecution have overtaken the promised land and have made home a land of "thorns and thistles."

THE POWER OF GOD AT HOME

New Creation

But the reference to first fruits reveals an even deeper hope that the garden may once again bear life. Again, the garden, the land, the temple, the very body of Christ and the outpouring of the Spirit, bear witness to God's presence. This presence of God brings a sense of new creation. In Paul's words, "So if anyone is in Christ, there is a new creation: everything old has passed away; see, everything has become new!" (2 Corinthians 5:17).

God's new creation is understood as being both here and not here. Or as some theologians put it, God's reign is "yet" and "not yet." Such an understanding helps us appreciate where the notion of the second coming of Christ, or the return of Christ, or the coming of God, or the kingdom coming itself comes from. In relation to this issue, no other book of the Bible has received more attention than the Book of Revelation, the last book of the New Testament, which lets us complete the biblical story line. Christians will probably always debate whether the book is a literal road map to the future, a symbolic prophetic appeal against injustice, or even the esoteric visions of a madman. But on this much most can agree: written in apocalyptic times, Revelation reveals the longing for God, especially in the midst of suffering. Revelation reveals the glimpse of hope in the midst of despair; it reveals the desire for life in a world full of death.

Seen in relation to the patterns of destruction and new life in the history of Israel, we can see a deep continuity. Revelation not only graphically portrays deep conflicts, battles, and warfare, it offers a glimpse of new life.

> Then I saw a new heaven and a new earth; for the first heaven and the first earth had passed away, and the sea was no more. And I saw the holy city, the new Jerusalem, coming down out of heaven from God, prepared as a bride adorned for her husband. And I heard a loud voice from the throne saying, "See, the home of God is among mortals. He will dwell with them as their God; they will be his peoples, and God himself will be with them; he will wipe every tear from their eyes. Death will be no more; mourning and crying and

pain will be no more, for the first things have passed away" [Revelation 21:1–4].

In this vision, which is so beautifully reminiscent of Isaiah 65, we glimpse the final hope, the purpose at work throughout the story of faith: *the home of God is among mortals.*

The vision in Revelation ends with a portrayal of a new Jerusalem. Only in this new Holy City there is no longer a temple. God and the Lamb of God *are* the temple, recalling the tight connection between Christ and the temple and the presence of God. Next in a passage strikingly similar to Ezekiel's vision of a temple, "Then the angel showed me the river of the water of life, bright as crystal, flowing from the throne of God and of the Lamb through the middle of the street of the city. On either side of the river is the tree of life with its twelve kinds of fruit, producing its fruit each month; and the leaves of the tree are for the healing of the nations" (Revelation 22:1–2).

So, as the Bible begins in the lush abundance of creation—a paradise—so it ends. Thistles and thorns are replaced by the river of life. Trees and their tempting fruit no longer symbolize death and curse but, instead, healing. And like my son who heard, "Come, David" in the night, instead of expulsion we have an invitation: "The Spirit and the bride say, 'Come.' And let everyone who hears say, 'Come.' And let everyone who is thirsty come. Let anyone who wishes take the water of life as a gift" (Revelation 22:17).

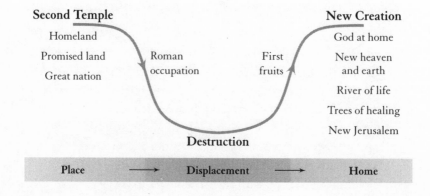

THE POWER OF GOD AT HOME

To appreciate the ways in which home, family life, congregations, and faith itself can be deep resources for children, it is helpful to immerse ourselves in the world of the sacred texts of our faith. The Bible puts an understanding of family and of home in the largest imaginable perspective. The Bible puts the struggles and hopes of living—all those plots we live daily—in the largest imaginable perspective. Underneath it all is a conviction: God is at home among mortals. This conviction sets the stage for considering what it might mean for God to be at home in our own particular lives, for God to be at home in the lives of our children.

Chapter 4

AN ABUNDANCE OF MEANING
How Faith Affects Vision

In the Book of Deuteronomy, Moses predicts that in a time to come children will ask, "What is the meaning of the decrees and the statutes and the ordinances that the LORD our God has commanded you?" Each generation has to learn not only the commands and ways of God but their meaning. Otherwise, as Moses saw, the decrees and statutes cannot be sustained. Each child, too, in a time to come, usually around adolescence, will ask, "Why? Why do we do this?" It is a good question, even a sign of maturity. But it can be a dreadful question for parents, especially because it often comes on the way out the door to services. The question is too big and too important to address in a hurry. The demand for quick answers reveals an adolescent's lingering immaturity.

Moses says that when children ask for meaning, tell them this: "We were Pharaoh's slaves in Egypt, but the LORD brought us out of Egypt with a mighty hand." And Moses continues to tell the history of Israel from slavery to the promised land. In other words, Moses says to tell them the story, for without it, religious commands and practices are lost. The story, the history, creates the larger perspective that gives ways of life meaning. Meaning, like learning, emerges in the relationship between part and whole. Without meaning we wither. So one of the hopes for raising children in the life of faith is that children will be in touch with deep and enduring sources of meaning and that they will thrive.

Katherine Paterson, the award-winning author of children's books, tells of growing up in China as a missionary kid. Her parents read and reread the stories of the Bible to her, "not to make us good," she says, "but to tell us who we were." She explains: "It is still hard for me to accept as fact that my blood ancestors were gentiles. . . . My real ancestors left Ur of the Chaldeans with Abraham and wandered in the wilderness with Moses."

Our tour through the scriptures only scratches the surface of this ancestry. Even so, it illustrates how important family and home have been in the history of faith. In turn, as Katherine Paterson suggests, the scriptures stretch the meaning of home and family by placing them in such a large perspective, that is, in relation to God. The Bible has this kind of power—the power to let us see in a larger context. The perspective is so wide. The time frame is so long. Our sense of the world expands. Our sense of life deepens. Family is not just nuclear; home is not just property.

Family is so much more. Family expands to include the generations, reaching into the ancient past for roots. The Bible stretches our imaginations as far back as possible to include even the first couple. At the same time, the scriptures also reveal a passionate concern for future generations. Teach the children. Listen and teach the children. Through children, the Bible reaches into the future for hope. In the process, our sense of who our brothers and sisters are expands as well. Our literal families become the foundation for our relationship to all of humanity. Family is ever more than blood or legal relationship.

Home is much more, too. The biblical sense of home reaches far into the past and way into the future. Home is homeland, a place to live, the place our ancestors lived, the promised land, the kingdom, the land for our descendants, the land flowing with milk and honey, even paradise. When considered against the backdrop of the Exodus in Egypt or the Exile in Babylon, home is also freedom. Our sense of home stretches all the way back to Eden and creation. It reaches forward to the new Jerusalem and the new creation. Literal home becomes the foundation for our relationship to creation itself. Home is ever more than property or shelter.

Given such a large perspective, it would nonetheless be a mistake to conclude that our smaller-scaled homes and our literal relationships do not matter. Blood, kinship, marriages, adoptions, as well as shelter, houses, apartments, gardens, and hometowns matter intensely. They matter in the same way literal touch matters to an infant or literal food matters to our bodies. Without concrete meaning, there can be no symbolic meaning. Without the literal, there can be no metaphor. As philosophers would put it, the Bible ties particulars with universals. The Bible ties a universal creation to the particular, promised place, Canaan. It ties universal parents to the particular household of Abraham and Sarah. Even the cosmic presence of God is tied to the specific temple. The Bible resists letting us think in single-minded ways: either too literally or too symbolically, too earthly or too heavenly. If we set our sights only on the big picture, if we get too heaven-minded, our attention is directed back to the earth in the form of Canaan, Israel, a child, or the doorposts of our homes. Here, right here, is wisdom, says Walter Brueggemann, "in the stuff of life, the world, our experience." Then again, if we cannot see beyond the doorposts of our own homes, if we think too narrowly, look only to immediate stuff, along comes a vision from heaven—a temple, a River of Life, or a new Jerusalem, to burst our insular bubbles. So not only learning, not only meaning, but wisdom itself involves this interplay between part and whole, between concrete stuff and a visionary imagination.

FAITH AND DEPTH PERCEPTION

I believe faith urges ever-deeper ways of seeing reality. Faith is born of a relationship to God or, perhaps more accurately, discovering God's relationship to us. The scriptures reveal a God passionate for our lives. In turn, God's passion awakens and calls forth human passion, like Abraham and Sarah for the promised land or the prophets' passion for justice. Faith deepens our sensitivity to life in all of life's grandeur and misery. Whether through a greater awareness of injustice or a deeper love for neighbor, either way faith engages us to life more fully. "I came that they may have life, and have it abundantly," says Jesus. This sense of abundance, this sense of fullness, this depth perception is crucial to appreciating the people and places of our hearts.

I have a pocketknife that to anyone else looks like a cheap old penknife good for peeling an apple, at best. My grandfather gave it to me when I was a young teenager. When I see it, I notice almost nothing of the knife's function or cost. More often than not, the scene of my grandfather and myself, sitting at our dining room table in the house where I grew up, flashes through my mind. There was a trick to opening the knife. At that time, I was a budding birthday-party magician. PaPa, as I called my grandfather, took great delight in watching me struggle to open it. After a lot of grins from tricking the young trickster, PaPa showed me how to open and close the blade, with care.

My grandfather died twenty-five years ago. So the knife is a treasure from another age for me. When I see the gift, I see more than I can even say. One slice of one dimension of a much greater relationship is connected to this simple object. Invisible to everyone else, all this is loaded into a gift thirty years old now. Yet through the magic of remembering, it could have been yesterday. The mystery of a relationship is that a simple little object like a pocketknife could be so loaded with meaning. It is a common knife; I, in fact, do peel apples with it all the time. It is also a treasure. The wonderful paradox is that the knife is both ordinary and extraordinary at the same time. The common and the treasured dwell together, flowing from a relationship between a grandfather and child that itself is ordinary and special. Relationships are like this.

Although relationship with God is certainly a unique kind of experience, some features of it are similar to other kinds of relations. Although what I see is invisible to others, I see much more in the object than just a knife. In the relationship of faith, we see the world with depth; we see the invisible at work in the visible. Through the ordinary elements of bread and wine, for example, we see relationship to an extraordinary God. In the bitter horseradish of a Passover Seder, there is the bitterness of Egyptian slavery. In the common water of baptism, there is the power of grace; in oil there is anointing.

Not only does faith help us "see" the world more fully but we feel it, smell it, hear it, and taste its elements. This does not imply that these simple things *only* appear this way (like a magician's illusion). We might see the world through rose-colored glasses, but the world is not really rose colored. No, the visible knife and the invisible relationship embedded in the history of the knife are both very real. Relationships are concrete through touch and communication and more. But relationships involve much that is not so visible—history, attitudes, values, or hopes, for example. Yet these are very real. They reflect depth in the relationship itself and consequently lend depth to the visible.

Faith involves the visible and invisible, and both are real. Relationship to an invisible God lends depth to our visible relationships, including the ones with our children. Faith has history, attitudes, values, and hopes, for example, born of this relationship. When the perspective born of faith is tied to the depth of our everyday relationships, meaning emerges. The relevance to raising children is this: God's love empowers a parent's love and reveals how ultimately meaningful love is.

THREATS TO MEANING

The spiritual life tries to stay in touch with meaning that endures. If meaning has to do with recognizing depth in living, meaninglessness, by this logic, has to do with flattening. If meaning has to do with fullness, meaninglessness is emptiness. In fact, people often use this kind of language to express meaninglessness: "The job has gone flat for me"; "I just feel empty"; "there's nothing there for us anymore." Sometimes these experiences of meaninglessness simply happen because of life's ups and downs. Losses of all kinds can breed them. But there are some persistent threats to meaning that are generated by life in this culture. Advertisements tell us that a new car, the latest computer, or the freshest beer will make our lives good. For the child, it is the newest toy, the sweetest candy bar, or the latest video game. It is not that these things are inherently bad. And it is not that most people really expect them to provide *ultimate* meaning (though some

An Abundance of Meaning

people come close). The temptation is more subtle. The temptation is to a manufactured dissatisfaction.

A consumer-oriented economy thrives on the continuous craving for more. It creates an atmosphere in which more is better, and it encourages dissatisfaction with what we have and who we are. It is a system that generates emptiness or exploits the ups and downs of life. A pervading sense of dissatisfaction and a gnawing feeling of meaninglessness actually help the cause of consumption. This kind of economy has had many successes, and it is not going away. But the spiritual danger is most intense when the atmosphere of consumption poses as the "whole" that is most important and promises salvation. When this happens, the meaning of other dimensions of life, such and home and family, are coopted for the sake of consumption. Families are to be good consumers and to produce good little consumers. In addition, values like giving, serving, or caring—values fundamental to family life—do not make much sense unless there is profit in it.

A second, related threat to meaning is woven into our passion for technology. A couple of years ago, I heard a promotional teaser for a news program that went something like this: "At the turn of the century, what is it that makes our homes home? We will look at toasters, dishwashers, televisions, and the other appliances that make where we live home." American culture's love of technology has provided many wonderful benefits. Not only do we make good gadgets, we constantly improve them, revealing what good problem solvers we are. We tackle a problem, reduce the situation to its most basic parts, then fix the flaw. If a car will not start, we check the elements of the starting system first—the battery, starter, or ignition—then we repair or replace the part.

Sometimes problem solving requires manipulating the whole system of parts and how they function together. A good research and development engineer for an automobile company might design a whole new starting system that replaces a conventional starter with something more reliable or efficient. This is the nature of progress. The goal is to make things more functional and more efficient. This can be quite good.

The Power of God at Home

But, as is true with consumption, the danger comes when the backside of technology is overlooked and technological goals overtake everything. When we look at life primarily through the lens of technology, what we see is perpetually dissatisfying. Nothing is efficient enough. Nothing is effective enough. It is one thing to be dissatisfied with the design of an automobile but quite another when dissatisfaction pervades deeper realms of life. Then families are never good enough, neither parents nor children. A technological point of view occludes depth, because depth leads to appreciation. And if we appreciate something, whether a book or pocketknife or parent or child, we are less likely to want to improve it. Therefore, when technology becomes the whole perspective, the parts are reduced to matters of function or efficiency. Home is a place for gadgets, a place for more efficient cooking or improved entertainment systems. Families are either functional or dysfunctional. Education is about getting a job. Religion is about—well, maybe it's not worth much. In such an atmosphere, meaning stands little chance of enduring. And this is dangerous. Lacking is the larger, deeper framework that helps us discern whether or not, for example, technological advances in cloning, euthanasia, or biological weapons are goals worth pursuing. (After all, the Nazis became notoriously effective and efficient at extermination—Hitler's solution to the Jewish "problem.") In the end, it may be a very good thing when our children ask "why" questions; at least something deep is stirring in them. Then again, if the questions are more like, "Why do we have to sit down at the table to eat together, I wanted to watch TV?" then the dissatisfaction of our age may be trying to creep in and flatten the lives of our children into techno-consumers.

Another major consequence of living in a highly technological society is a general scattering of attention. Consider the impact of e-mail, telephones, watches, televisions, radios, cars, planes, Palm Pilots, pagers, the Web, commercials, faxes, PowerPoint, and whatever must-have device or software comes next. Any one of these things can be great. Who can argue against the joy of getting a phone call or e-mail from a long-lost friend or a relative overseas? Looking at the parts alone is to miss the overall impact of immersion in electronic media. In a world so saturated, it is getting tough to concentrate or pay attention for very long. Yet—and this is the larger point—both learning and meaning demand sustained attention. Meaningful family life demands sustained attention to one another. In our own family, we have finally had to take the telephone off the hook during meals and turn the cell phone off during family vacations.

A friend of mine from church told me how her family (including two teenagers) has begun having breakfast together. Instead of each person grabbing something on the run, as they always had, the whole family actually sits down together on work days and school days, in one place at the same time, as the sun rises; they read from the first chapter of Genesis. Each day, they read about one day of creation and how God saw it was good, very good. I asked about this, and the friend told me, "Everything around us tries to tell us to be cynical and dissatisfied, so taking even five minutes, including our time to eat, to know goodness, to look at each other face-to-face, has got to be worth something." Over and over again, daily, they read of the goodness of God's creative work and welcome the day with appreciation. "Breakfast itself has become meaningful to us now, in ways it never had been." This family, maybe intuitively, discovered at least a partial antidote to the perpetual dissatisfaction, cynicism, distraction, and danger always knocking at the door. The story of God's good creation feeds the soul of this family with meaning, as food feeds their bodies.

Unless technological and consumer values are located within and are limited by a deeper, more enduring set of values, we are left flat and empty. A vicious cycle ensues; we do more, pursue more, yet it means less and less. I believe the world of faith gives power over these temptations by helping us know what is ultimately valuable. Teaching children to see through the false promises and thin claims of the world around them is much easier when parents can point to and live by a view of the world that recognizes creative goodness. Instead of an insatiable pursuit of more stuff, more is seen in the stuff of life. There is still plenty of room for technology, problem solving, and material goods, but they are located within larger concerns. Maybe technology could be employed to actually empower the disenfranchised. Maybe we can better tackle the problem of world hunger or domestic violence. Who needs what goods in our community? There is plenty to be genuinely dissatisfied about, and there are lots of important problems to solve. But faith is a perspective large enough to differentiate meaningful dissatisfaction from manufactured ones.

HOLINESS

The word *holy* has come upon hard times. It has come to mean a kind of hypermorality: "Oh, he acts so holier-than-thou." But this is a distortion of the word. Nearly a hundred years ago, theologian Rudolf Otto, in a book titled *The Idea of the Holy,* made it clear that such an understanding is inadequate. He explained that biblically and theologically, the idea of the holy instead refers to "a clear overplus of meaning." Otto uses the phrase *mysterium tremendum* to refresh our ears to this sense of holiness. The phrase carries a sense of the tremendous, the awesome, and the majestic. "The Holy" could create a sweeping feeling like a gentle tide, or it could burst forth suddenly, Otto says; it could lead to ecstasy on the one hand or horror, depending on the form. Holiness could also be beautiful and glorious.

C. S. Lewis presents a wonderful glimpse into this sense of *mysterium tremendum* through his tale for children, *The Lion, the Witch, and the Wardrobe.* Four children find themselves in Narnia, an enchanted land full of talking creatures and magic. Aslan, the lion, is a messianic figure in the story. A beaver tells the children, "They say Aslan is on the move, perhaps has already landed." The narrator then says,

> None of the children knew who Aslan was any more than you do; but the moment the Beaver had spoken these words everyone felt quite different. Perhaps it has sometimes happened to you in a dream that someone says something which you don't understand but in the dream it feels as if it had some enormous meaning—either a terrifying one which turns the

An Abundance of Meaning

whole realm into a nightmare or else a lovely meaning too lovely to put into words, which makes the dream so beautiful that you remember it all your life and are always wishing you could get into that dream again. It was like that now.

Even the name of Aslan in the story was enough to evoke a mysterious sense of awe. Yet the reaction to this sense depended on the situation of each child. Each felt something different at the name of Aslan.

Edmund [who had betrayed the others] felt a sensation of mysterious horror. Peter felt suddenly brave and adventurous. Susan felt as if some delicious smell or some delightful strain of music had just floated by her. And Lucy got the feeling you have when you wake up in the morning and realize that it is the beginning of the holidays or the beginning of summer.

Though it was a fantasy, Lewis was drawing on his own faith and a sense of holiness (that he also wrote about in other, nonfiction forms). As Otto puts it, to experience *mysterium tremendum* is to be "in the presence of that which is a *mystery* inexpressible." *Mystery* here is not just something we cannot figure out (that is the way we use the term in a technological society). Mystery comes from the Greek root *mystos,* which means "keeping silence." The idea is that mysteries evoke silence not because we cannot know anything but because we know more than we can capture in words. We encounter something that creates a "hushed, trembling, and speechless humility." To put it into words too easily endangers reducing the "overplus of meaning."

Holiness attracts, on the one hand, but overwhelms on the other. Before leading the Israelites out of slavery, Moses encountered a burning bush in the desert. He was attracted by it and went to look. But then the LORD said, "Come no closer! Remove the sandals from your feet, for the place on which you are standing is holy ground." Moses hid his face, afraid to look at God (Exodus 3:4–6). Holiness invites us near but only with the deepest forms of respect. Even the name of God that Moses receives reflects this sense of the Holy: "I AM WHO I AM." In the original Hebrew language, the name comes from the root "to be." Implied in the name is this: I will be who I will be—you cannot control me. In addition, the name is not to be spoken. Orthodox Jews to this day, as well as many translations of the Bible (as I have used in this book), use the word *LORD* instead of the original Hebrew word out of reverence.

Although some, unfortunately, would call this superstition or magical thinking, I believe the practice of respecting the name of God like this actually flows from a deep sense of respect for the Holy. Implied is a sense that God is more than we can say, evoking hushed humility. Admittedly, this is a kind of paradox. God reveals on the one hand but conceals on the other. God is both present and hidden simultaneously. The LORD appears, but is more. And as a result, Moses is, on the one hand, made humble, taking off his sandals and hiding his face, and is empowered on the other, returning to Egypt to confront the mighty Pharaoh.

Burning bush experiences of the Holy do not happen every day, obviously, but nonetheless they can affect the way one approaches everyday living. Awareness of the Holy and of the empowered, yet humble, posture it creates can spill over into everyday living. Genesis says as much: creation emerges from the breath of God, and the first human emerges when the LORD breathes life into dust. Genesis is saying God's breath, God's Spirit, God's holiness permeates life. Not only the Creator, not only the human creature, but creation too is more than a technological problem, more than we can say. "To live only on that which we can say is to wallow in the dust," writes Abraham Heschel, intensely aware of holiness. "How shall we ignore the mystery, in which we are involved, to which we are attached by our very existence? How shall we remain deaf to the throb of the cosmic that is subtly echoed in our own souls?" And Heschel answers, "Wonder alone is the compass that may direct us to the pole of meaning." Not only are holiness and meaning tightly related; so is wonder.

An Abundance of Meaning

Radical Amazement

Wonder is our guide. Wonder reveals the meaning at work in the universe. One of the most profound experiences of wonder in my own life occurred soon after the birth of our daughter Cora. There was, of course, the incredibly hard work of pregnancy, labor, and delivery on Jane's part. However, there were no complications, no extra worries, no medical problems. Mother and daughter were exhausted but in good health. After lots of holding and tears and smiles, maybe an hour or so later, while Jane rested and a nurse and I were cleaning Cora, something hit me. I was entranced by my daughter's sheer presence. The sense of wonder overcame me, beyond words, beyond tears even. She and the room even seemed to glow. The nurse, wiping my daughter's precious body, gently commented, "You have to believe in God, don't ya?" I think the nurse saw the glow, too.

I realize that experiences of intense wonder around birth, and adoption as well, are not that unusual for parents. But that makes the case all the more strongly. Rabbi Heschel calls it "radical amazement." In wonder or radical amazement "each thing is a surprise, *being is unbelievable.*" Not only are we amazed with the things in life around us, "we are amazed at seeing anything at all, . . . at the fact there is being at all." Wonder, mystery, holiness—they are all around us, even in us. We may not always see them, but they are there all the same.

In the past several years, I have asked hundreds of students, of all ages, to write about and share such experiences of wonder or radical amazement. Striking is the fact that no one has ever said, "I can't think of anything." That fact alone reveals something. For some, these are explicitly religious experiences, occurring in some kind of religious context; for others, they are not necessarily so, not directly anyway. It is more like wonder will be where it will be. Always, people say the experience is more than they can fully describe in words, yet the words have a way of bringing some of the power of the experience back. In addition, I am always struck by how tied to the sensory world such experiences are: autumn leaves or a colorful sky, towering mountains or a field of grass, brilliant stars or birds singing at dawn, warm breezes on the skin or the sight of the ocean. The human-oriented world is often described as well: sanctuaries and hospitals, homes and

THE POWER OF GOD AT HOME

ice cream parlors, stadiums and parks, families and crowds, babies and friends, too. These intense, extraordinary experiences do not take people out of life. Wonder is not out of the world; we do not take leave of our senses. On the contrary, wonder throws people into life even more abundantly. It is more accurate to say that people's senses are sharpened and awareness is intensified. Attention is riveted.

MYSTERY AND MEANING

What does this have to do with children and families? With home? With faith? My concern is that the heavy value placed on functioning, efficiency, output, and problem solving in Western societies creates cataracts in our vision of life. The result is that our senses dull. Awareness fades. Appreciation dims. And meaning fades away.

Tragically, these cataracts affect our culture's understandings of family as well. Families are just this or families are just that. Families should look like this or should be like that. The problem with families today is this or the problem is that. It is as if just defining families would let us figure them out, control them, manage or fix them. On the battle lines of the culture wars, we obsess over images of family on television, in textbooks, or in the movies. But this obsession only reveals that our appreciation of them has become as flat as a television screen. These are family facades. These are cultural idols reducing the abundance of life.

I believe the world of faith works in a different direction. Faith deepens life, widens perspective, and intensifies awareness. Faith is in touch with mystery. The philosopher Gabriel Marcel has written as powerfully as anyone on the topic of *mystery*. Like Otto's *mysterium tremendum,* a mystery is not simply an unsolved problem. It is much more. Problems can be figured out. Problems can be solved with the right method; they are reducible to a set of categories or formulas. Problems are to be fixed. Instead, for Marcel life is a mystery precisely because there is always more to life than could ever be figured out. Meaning overflows.

To approach life as *problem* is a framework of controlling power. And like any approach to living, this framework carries its own sense of right and wrong. The moral life is generated from what we value, from where our hearts are. Marcel used the example of a sleeping child to illustrate the difference between problem and mystery and their different moral frameworks. From the point of view of power, "the sleeping child is completely unprotected and appears to be utterly *in our power*; from that point of view, it is permissible for us to do what we like with the child." This is the true mark of barbarism, according to Marcel. "But from the point of view of mystery, we might say that it is just because this being is completely unprotected, that it is utterly at our mercy, that it is also invulnerable or sacred." Barbaric morality refuses to recognize or value this sacredness. In other words, mystery generates its own sense of right and wrong. To approach others as mysteries is to recognize their sacredness. They are not to be reduced, ridiculed, or manipulated. That is wrong. To approach others as mysteries is to sense the breath of God in them—that which is irreducible, beyond words, or deeper than linear categories. Your children are mysteries. You are a mystery.

Mysteries evoke wonder. Mysteries evoke respect. They draw out a sense of the precious. Mystery is another way of talking about holiness. Others are ever more than we could exhaust with our words, concepts, ideologies, or stereotypes. As Craig Dykstra, relying on Marcel, puts it, "People are mysteries, and being moral means treating them as such. Our world is a mystery, and being moral means encountering it that way. At the depth of being there is an Ultimate Mystery, and being moral means being properly related to that Mystery." Faith—our connection to Ultimate Mystery—opens onto an inexhaustible reality: abundant life. Wonder, holiness, sacredness, awe, mystery, radical amazement, meaning, and morality flow. Abundant life is both life everlasting and a profound awareness of mystery now. From sleeping children to sanctuaries, faith evokes reverence. From temples to our bodies, wherever the Spirit of God dwells, there is the power of mystery.

Kathleen Deyer-Bolduc has written a devotional book about raising her child who has disabilities. The book is called *His Name Is Joel*. In it, she tells of some frustrating experiences she was having with the Sunday school of her congregation, which culminated in a meeting with the Sunday school director. "We need to know more about Joel," the director said to her, trying to be helpful. "Tell us about his diagnosis, his I.Q., his learning style, his behavioral problems. . . . Let's attack this problem as a team." She goes on to explain,

> We talked for over an hour before it dawned on me. We were discussing a "problem," rather than Joel. "I wish you really knew Joel," I said passionately. "All you see are the outward manifestations of his disability—the hair pulling, the short attention span, the difficulties in learning. Under all of that is a very precious little boy with strengths as well as weaknesses."

Faith stretches our minds and hearts toward such a large and deep perspective. But in light of mystery, we can see that this stretching is not to make us smarter than others, not to make us stronger than others. Faith empowers, but in its own way: to have the eyes to see others as mysteries and treat them accordingly. Faith evokes the sense of irreducible sacredness, even in little boys and girls who don't fit norms, who don't function at the same levels, who may never outgrow their stages. Yet enfolded by loving relationships, such so-called *problems* are recognized as what they truly are: *mysteries.*

FAMILIES AS MYSTERIES

Families are mysteries. In fact, in a beautiful passage reflecting on mystery, Dykstra says that "people are mysteries" because "we cannot get them taped down, secured, and under control." Continuing this idea, I suggest that we can substitute the word *families* for *people.* Families are mysteries because "we cannot get them taped down, secured, and under control." The quote continues,

> There is always more to them than we can comprehend. . . . There are depths to them that, as we come to know them more fully, are opened up to us—often in surprising and delightful ways, but also at times in frightful and disorienting ways. In any case, it is just their uniqueness . . . that makes [families] mysteries—and treasures.

Describing families this way is not arbitrary. In fact, Marcel's earliest published example of mystery is the mystery of family. To see families as mysteries is to see them in the light of faith. Families are charged with meaning, sometimes for better and sometimes for worse, but charged nonetheless. But to treat a family as simply an institution that can be manipulated by propaganda and politics is to reduce family to a problem. To treat families purely as problems to be fixed is to degrade their spiritual possibilities. This is the nature of evil, according to Marcel. Evil is the act of degrading mysteries to problems.

A Real Family Life

As Katherine Paterson suggests, we read the Bible to discover who we are. Faith opens depths to ourselves by connecting us to our ancestors, by connecting us to our Creator even. Significantly, we learn that others have depths as well, including families, including children, including our own families and children. Such learning thickens life with meaning.

With all the debates about family values swirling about in the media and politics these days, it can be difficult to generate genuine, thoughtful ideas and practices in relation to actual families. To some, families are all problems, dysfunctional in nearly every way. To others, families are the key to our salvation as a nation. When I listen to the debates, I get a very queasy feeling that families, real families, are not the true subject. Such polarized debates have a way of distorting our vision. Popular culture often does the same. Families are portrayed either as all things bright and beautiful or all things dull and ugly. It is as if sweetness and cynicism are our only options.

One of the goals of this book is to explore ways of seeing family life as real, as it truly is. Home can be grand; it can be miserable. Families can bless children; they can curse children. Inevitably families do both, and more. So we look by faith.

Chapter 5

WHAT GOES WRONG?

If there is so much wonder and holiness around—in us, in creation, in our children—what happens? The previous chapter describes the depth perception of faith. This perception, this vision, reveals wonder, mystery, and holiness. Education in the context of faith, then, is learning to see the world against such an amazing background, that is, connecting the parts to this grand whole. Spiritual learning in the context of family life is connecting the parts of our lives to the Holy. Of course we don't always. And worse, family life can take terrible turns. In fact, religion itself can go terribly wrong. Any realm that involves relationships—from homes and congregations to neighborhoods and nations—can get so twisted that we have to call it evil. Family violence, manipulative cults, sexual predation, and genocide—all illustrate Gabriel Marcel's description of evil as turning mysteries into problems. They all involve being blind to the depths of others and treating them accordingly.

As unpleasant as it is, spiritual training involves getting an angle on sin, that is, learning to see what goes wrong in the world, in ourselves even, and helping the next generation do so as well. To address sin is to address some of the hardest questions of all: Why do we hurt one another? How can people be so mean? Why did I do that? The pain that we can cause one another is too great to ignore, as parents and as people of faith. On the one hand, the destructive possibilities of sin run deep; they are powerful and our children are vulnerable. On the other hand, awareness of our destructive possibilities heightens the importance of faith itself. Faith is power against sin. If we can help give our children, not to mention ourselves, a solid place to stand in the middle of the snares and dangers of life, there could be no greater gift.

The first task is recognizing the temptations. Rather than thinking of sin simply as breaking rules, I am suggesting that sin is often not so easy to see; it is slippery and deceptive. Sin is often more of a twisting than a breaking, and that is what makes it both deceptive and powerful. Sin takes relationships that are otherwise good and turns them around in destructive ways. It could be a relationship with another person; it could be relationship with God. But sin feeds off the power of relationships like a parasite on a host and uses that power for its own deadly purposes. And because family life is such an intense and potentially good form of relationship, there is extra incentive to pay attention to the ways sin twists the good of family relationships. Rather than the power and beauty of picking up God's rhythms, as Norman Maclean describes the life of faith, sin disempowers, and it is ugly.

The ways in which relationships get ugly and in which sin disempowers are multiple, but I have found three general categories of sin that are helpful for noticing when that happens. Like the plot I offered for the Bible, sin is ever more complex than these categories, but I hope they give us a way into this complexity. Drawing on the deeply insightful reflections of theologian Edward Farley, the three basic temptations are (1) escapism, (2) idolatry, and (3) manipulation. These temptations are related to each other, and they threaten any kind of relationship, from nations relating to nations to parents relating to children—even to an individual relating to him- or herself. Whereas escapism has to do with running away from commitments and relationships, idolatry has to do with overcommitment to the wrong things. Manipulation, in turn, has to do with using and misusing others. And while these temptations are present at all levels of human existence, the challenge of raising children and living in families makes the stakes immediate and personal. If, however, sin twists the good, I want to be clear about the good that gets turned around. What is the good that goes sour?

THE POWER OF GOD AT HOME

GOD'S IMAGE

The first chapter of Genesis describes God's creation of humanity: "So God created humankind in his image, in the image of God he created them; male and female he created them" (1:27). This is the background preceding the particular creation of Adam and Eve. Humanity is made in God's image. This is quite an affirmation—one that evokes respect for the human creature. "God saw everything that he had made," verse 30 continues, "and indeed it was very good."

It is no accident that those I quoted earlier regarding depth and mystery (Otto, Marcel, Heschel, Dykstra, Deyer-Bolduc) are all people of faith thoroughly embedded in this affirmation. Faith not only has a vision of God but faith has a vision of humanity. People reflect God. Biblically, humanity is not valued simply because of its work. People are not respected because they work well or communicate clearly or behave perfectly—not at all. Having righteous characters is not the basis for this image. In fact, the Bible brilliantly reveals what flawed and misguided characters we so often are. Disobedience, blaming, jealously, and even murder happen within the very first family. But this only makes the claim all the more poignant. Pulsing beneath the "damned mess" of humanity (as Norman Maclean's father put it), God's image remains. Irreducible. Inherently valuable. Faith helps us see this reflection.

Historically, theologians have seen a close relationship between the image of God in humanity and human freedom. Recall that the name of God given to Moses implied, "I will be who I will be." Implicit was a promise: "I will be there." But there was also a warning, "Don't try to control me." God is free. Likewise, those made in the image of God are free. God is not reducible to our plans and projects; the Holy One transcends this world, is beyond, is free from our control. This tells us something about those creatures made in God's image. There is a reflection of that transcendence in humanity as well. We are not made to be controlled by others. We are made free.

Freedom is part of our "wonderfully strange" nature that I mentioned in Chapter One. We are bodily creatures full of instincts and

What Goes Wrong?

needs and survival mechanisms, but we appear less tightly tied to them than other creatures are. There is more. We can suppress urges for immediate gratification for the sake of larger goals. We can do this, or we can do that. I can take that path or this one; you can work for this goal or a completely different one. We can imagine radically different alternatives and choose among them. This is powerful. We can even choose whether to be or not. This is to say that our instincts are not simply a closed loop of stimulus and response. They are open to creative transformations even. For example, the urge to reproduce and care for our own biological children (getting our genes into another generation, as biologists put it) does not have to be met literally. We can love and care for adopted children or stepchildren. Or love and care can be devoted to a whole classroom of children, to a congregation's children, to a whole society's children. The relative freedom from instincts can lead to freedom for creative possibilities. In other words, our lives are open to possibilities, and in that openness emerges the freedom to choose how to live. By contrast, the Bible also portrays the alternative to this freedom: slavery. Biblically, the Pharoah and his slavery were the antithesis of the LORD and freedom. The Exodus is not only an important part of the past but it reveals part of what it means to be created in God's image now. We are made to be who we will be.

In addition to freedom, there is another dimension to God reflected in humanity. God not only transcends the world but God is present to it. The Creator loves creation. Theologian Jürgen Moltmann emphasizes that creation itself is an expression of God's passion for relationship. Out of infinite love, God brings into being that which is other than God. Why? To love. Creation is for love's sake. Creation is even a kind of communion, like a family, inherently inter-relational. "Everything exists, lives and moves *in others,* in one another, for one another, in the cosmic interrelations of the divine Spirit." We are made in the image of this God. We are made for love, for relationship, for communion with God, and for community with one another. We are made to engage in life with others. So another side of our open nature is that we are open to relationship. Some theologians have even called this another side of freedom. Not only are we free *from* control or slavery but we are *for* relationship. This is our nature and, in the words of Genesis, it is good (full of possibilities).

There is a third aspect to our open nature and what it means to be made in God's image. That is creativity. God is the Creator and endows humanity with creative powers. "Be fruitful and multiply" were God's first words to humanity. But this fruitfulness is not limited to biological reproduction. We can create in so many ways. We can create something where there was nothing; we can create crops in fields, or buildings and temples, or whole cities and nations. We can create tools, languages, music, sculptures, novels, paintings, poems, and philosophies. We can take the stuff of life—sometimes visible like dirt or paint, sometimes invisible like ideas or fictional characters—and make it into something new. We can even create with the stuff of our own lives, through choices, imagination, and relationships.

OUR WONDERFULLY STRANGE NATURES

Creativity relies heavily on freedom and relationship. The lines between creativity, freedom, and relationship should not be drawn too sharply because all three constantly work together to generate life. They are really just three perspectives on our wonderfully strange natures, three dimensions of the mystery of our lives. But they are three dimensions that provide an angle on what can go wrong. In fact, it is when freedom, love, and creativity are wrenched away from one another that trouble broods. Sin, from this point of view, is a distortion of the powers made possible by our natures. Sin dims the reflection of the Creator God, the LORD, the Passionate God in us. Sin flattens and empties the fullness of mystery. I am suggesting three basic kinds of distortion, corresponding to these three dimensions of the image of God. Surely there are more, but these cover a lot of ground.

Escapism

A major challenge for those of us raising teenagers is trying to help them understand that the freedom they push for carries a lot of responsibility. From staying up or out later to driving a car to dating, freedom requires maturity. Like any power, it must be handled with care, or it will explode. And this is the point in relation to sin. The very same nature that opens possibilities and choice allows us to choose badly or to wind up around others who do so, wronging us. Freedom lets humanity be destructive, hurtful, and manipulative, as the Bible makes so very clear. In other words, the power of freedom can lead to incredible good and inexpressible evil alike.

Escapism is a distortion of freedom. The same good freedom that allows us to break away from destructive situations—the freedom that set the Israelites free from Egypt, for example—allows us to run away indefinitely. We can run from commitments, flee responsibilities, bail out on our loved ones, even abandon ourselves. Escapism sprints away from the engaged life of dwelling. The nineteenth-century philosopher and theologian Søren Kierkegaard called such avoidance a "flight from actuality into the desert." On the one hand, a person can flee relationships by avoiding and undermining them. On the other, one can flee figuratively by remaining self-enclosed, even in the midst of relationships. For Kierkegaard, without the concreteness of genuine relationships and all the entanglements that love requires, we never become real. This is despair, rooted in fear. If you think of the "fight or flight" response in animals, escapism in human beings is a kind of perpetual flight, even when there is no threat. We keep our distance (transcend, fly above) the earthier bogs of relationship. Escape is everything.

Nothing in life is immune from this temptation, even the spiritual life. Spirituality, religion, and ministry, for example, can even become escapist. I worry that most popular images of spirituality and ministry run precisely in the opposite direction of the earthier dimensions of family living or raising children. Deserts, mountaintops, sanctuaries, pulpits, monasteries, monks, ministers, robes, rabbis, silence, order, calm, light, and serenity mark typical notions of spirituality. Significantly, these images suggest distance from the ordinary, everyday world. The implied idea is that getting nearer to God means distancing ourselves from the ordinary. The idea is that really spiritual people get out of life to get into God more fully, get out of the mundane to get into the Divine.

Ernest Boyer tells the story in his book, *A Way in the World,* of an experience he had at Harvard Divinity School. He heard a lecture on "the spirituality of the desert," that is, how the monks of early Christianity left their homes for the caves of the Egyptian desert in order to devote themselves to the life of solitary prayer and contemplation. Boyer said he found the description compelling and discovered his own attraction to such a spirituality. Yet as a husband and father, he also felt frustrated. "Was such a life possible with the commitment of a family?" he asked himself. After class, out of his conflicted feelings, he finally went to the professor. "Just one question," he said. "Is there childcare in the desert?"

Indeed, powerful religious events and moments do happen on mountaintops and in the wilderness and among people who have removed themselves from the everyday trivialities of life to make room for something more holy. But this is one-sided if homes and communities are left in the dust. In fact, the desert monks did have deep human relationships and created new forms of community. The story has more to do with images of the spiritual life and the dissonance between those images and the demands of parenting. Somehow wiping the noses and bottoms of our baby sons and daughters does not fit. Somehow wiping the noses and bottoms of our aging fathers or grandmothers does not square with popular images of the spiritual life. Yet if life in the Spirit is a life of loving communion with others, how can we escape such care?

I hope I am clear: freedom is good. It is crucial to life and makes us unique and interesting. But wrenched from a larger vision of who we are and what life is about, the very good can become very bad. This is part of sin's deception: escapism masks as freedom, making it hard to recognize the distortion. In societies and cultures that prize individual freedom, for example, the benefits of individual liberty make recognizing the dangers even more difficult. Western culture generally, in the last few centuries, has increasingly understood freedom in terms of individual liberties and legal rights. The emphasis on freedom has brought rights to individuals and groups who had none, has helped abolish all kinds of slavery, and now keeps a persistent check on the power of governments. These illustrate the good power of freedom. But new dangers are created in this atmosphere, ones relevant to both family and congregational life. The place of community, roots, family, and relationships generally recedes while autonomy, individualism, and greed move forward.

In the passionate book by Sylvia Ann Hewlett and Cornel West, *The War Against Parents,* the authors describe the devastating consequences that such an emphasis on individual autonomy can create. "Unchecked radical individualism has produced a society in which people are increasingly unable to sustain relationships or look after their young." Therefore, the authors spell out, family and community life suffer. "We can't have our cake and eat it: unlimited choice and uncluttered freedom get in the way of family strength and community well-being." The issues come to a head in parenting. Parenting, like any nurturing activity, requires the ability to look after and care for others. Parenting, for men and women alike, requires the ability to get out of oneself and to connect, to attach, to serve, and to watch out for others as well as oneself. This ability to connect is not only crucial for the child or for the family's well-being but Hewlett and West reveal the significance for the larger society. When the deep connection between parent and child weakens, there is a devastating impact on the nation, "for the sacrificial, other-directed work that parents do is the wellspring of compassion, competence, and commitment in society." In other words, when freedom is distorted at the expense of commitment and responsibility, it explodes on us, making relationships, community life, and families difficult to sustain. Whole societies can become blind to the most vulnerable in our midst, deaf to the cries of those who need care and commitment more than any. Escapism is not simply an individual act or lifestyle; societies can cultivate an atmosphere that makes caring for others difficult.

In one way, escapism could be understood as freedom without relationship. This would be like a god who will be who god wants to be but who does not hear the cries of the people who are suffering (as the LORD, indeed, heard). With escapism, distance takes perpetual priority over nearness. Getting away overrides getting close. Detachment overrules attachment. In these cases, whether discussing a god, parent, or society, freedom escapes relationships.

THE POWER OF GOD AT HOME

But what about the reverse? Is it possible to attach too much, get too close, or commit too much? Can the otherwise good capacity for relationship get twisted?

Idolatry

Our openness for relationship lets us attach and commit to one another in deep and powerful ways. This is good; it is part of our nature. Our capacity for relationship and love is necessary for family life and parenting, but it lets us relate to God in deep and powerful ways as well. But what if we attach deeply to the wrong things? What if we get overcommitted? This is idolatry. Idolatry is misplaced worship. If escapism cannot get close, idolatry cannot get away. If escapism lets go of relationships and commitments too easily, idolatry holds on to them too tightly, choking out life. Once again, sin, from this point of view, is trickier than rule violation; it is worse. Sin twists the good and wounds life in the process. Idols do so in the most deceptive ways. They promise salvation on the surface, but they create slavery. Money, drugs, career, sex, and power can all be good things until they start promising too much. Overattachment, overcommitment, and overinvestment in any of these goods can twist them into gods and our lives into their service. Here's how it might go: my life revolves around money or the pursuit of money; I can't get enough of it; I'll work even more for it, sacrifice time at home for more of it, or gamble until I hit it big. The same scenario could be created for work, for recognition, for attention, for a cause, or even human relationships.

Because we are social creatures, the fallout of idolatry is not isolated to an individual's own behavior; there are social consequences. The somewhat overused term *codependency* originally referred to the ways in which the friends and family members around an alcoholic get caught in the compulsions and destruction, even if they do not themselves drink. Spouses, children, and friends, trying to cope, find ways to survive. A child acts more like a parent than the parent; a spouse calls the alcoholic's boss to say he or she is sick and won't be at work; these behaviors make it easier for the alcoholic to drink. So a vicious cycle is at work. Self-destructive lifestyles generate a lot of instability and insecurity. But insecurity can make change even more difficult. Self-destructive patterns of living offer a kind of security, even if it is false security. In other words, idolatry resists change, even when the change is liberating. Everyone around the alcoholic, not just the alcoholic, is bowing down to the god. So, as it is with freedom, something good about our natures—the capacity for relationship, for attaching and caring—gets twisted and tangled into a shadowy version of itself.

We can notice, then, that idolatry undoes freedom. Idols make you believe that if you stop bowing to them, if you let go or change, life will be even worse. True worship, however, generates both freedom and caring. Why do we worship the LORD? Deuteronomy asks. Because the LORD brought us out, set us free from Egypt, and brought us to the land of our ancestors. So, although freedom without attachment is escapist, attachment without freedom is slavery.

An idol, according to Psalm 115, is that which is made by human hands.

> Their idols are silver and gold, the work of human hands. They have mouths, but do not speak; eyes, but do not see. They have ears, but do not hear; noses, but do not smell. They have hands, but do not feel; feet, but do not walk; they make no sound in their throats. Those who make them are like them; so are all who trust in them [4–8].

The psalmist is warning us that idols are simply human constructions. They are parts, not the whole. Or more accurately, idols are parts that mask as the whole. Instead of enlarging and deepening our sense of life, they lessen it. Idols make us senseless. They perpetually offer the promise of salvation but never deliver; they only ask for more. In this way, anything on earth can offer such a false promise. Even families and children, even ideas, education, or religion can become idolatrous. A conception of God, for example, that is too narrow, can even become a false god. How? Unlike God, a concept has no freedom, no transcendence, if we grasp it too tightly. Our tightly held conception cannot say, "I will be who I will be." An image of God becomes more important than who God actually is. And we can do the same to our families or children. Images of them become more important than who they actually are.

The same capacity that allows me to recognize a universe of meaning in a pocketknife is the same capacity that allows me to over-invest my life's meaning in something. The fear of losing the knife could lead me to cling too tightly to it. It is like the story of the man who all of a sudden became rich, then cannot sleep for fear of losing his money. Idolatry narrows our vision. The idol says, "Look at me, look at me, look only at me!" We lose a bigger picture.

The family therapist and author Salvador Minuchin has noticed how family members interact with each other along a continuum of closeness and distance. He used the terms *enmeshed* and *disengaged* to identify extreme closeness or extreme distance in families. Whereas most families fall somewhere in between or move back and forth with ease for different circumstances, sometimes families get stuck in patterns that make family living difficult. Enmeshment is an example of a closeness that makes individuality very difficult. If something happens to one person, it happens to everyone. If one is upset, all will be upset. "The parents in an enmeshed family may become tremendously upset because a child does not eat his dessert." Or in disengaged families, if something happens to one member, it doesn't matter. There is so much individuality that there is little sense of community. For example, "The parents in a disengaged family may feel unconcerned about a child's hatred of school."

In one case, there is an emotional clinging, a holding on so tightly that it chokes individuality, that it quashes uniqueness, that it overwhelms the relationship itself. In the other case, there is so much letting go that there is little care, not enough concern; community itself cannot emerge. A relationship requires both individuality and community, difference and common concern, the freedom to be unique and the passion to care. Families are continuously working out or negotiating (not necessarily intentionally) how close to get to one another, how much space to give each other, and what the possibilities are. The educational point is that these everyday patterns of living are the soil in which children are growing and learning and discovering what it means to be a person. And the theological point is that our relationship to God is the soil for learning about freedom and love.

Manipulation

The third area of distortion has to do with creativity. We are made in the image of the Creator, and creativity is a fruit of our open nature. We can generate new life, new ideas, new ways of being. This is power. We can make things; we can make things happen. Our creative powers allow us to experiment, to move things around in new ways. We can craft beautiful objects from raw materials, or we can produce fields of grain from soil and seeds. Creativity is related to other aspects of our nature, to freedom and love. To create we have to imagine, by freedom, new possibilities. To create, we have to work with the stuff of life, engaging it respectfully.

However, when creativity is wrenched apart from freedom and love, it becomes something other than "good." Tragically, human beings can be creatively destructive. I am calling this manipulation. Manipulation moves things around for destructive purposes, typically stealing freedom from others or undercutting their good relationships. I am talking about all the ways people use people, abuse them, terrorize, tyrannize, intimidate, or eliminate them. The Pharaoh manipulated the Israelites in Egypt for making bricks. American agriculture manipulated Africans and their descendants for economic gain. In both cases, freedom was lost and slaves were cut off from home.

As is the case with escapism and idolatry, manipulation can take so many forms and sour so many realms of living. We can manipulate physically, emotionally, spiritually, or psychologically. And manipulation can happen wherever relationships are—in families, in congregations, at work, in politics, or on the playground at school, for example. Bullies can manipulate with fists, teachers with ideas and grades, pastors with salvation, or nations with weapons. Wherever a lot of power is granted a person or position, especially over the well-being of others, the temptations are particularly intense and dangerous, for example, among leaders, lawmakers, clergy, caregivers, or parents. The vulnerability of others heightens the responsibility of those with power. Citizens are vulnerable before the law, for example, and children are vulnerable with adults. Vulnerability intensifies the risk of manipulation.

As we saw in the scriptures, the prophets were particularly concerned with abuses of power among the kings. Recall that King David even manipulated his army so that the soldier Uriah would be killed, leaving his widow Bathsheba for the king. It took the prophet Nathan to condemn this manipulation. According to the prophets, even worship of God, if cut off from concern for the vulnerable (widows and orphans are often mentioned), are vain attempts to manipulate God. Through the prophet Amos, God says:

> I hate, I despise your festivals, and I take no delight in your solemn assemblies. Even though you offer me your burnt offerings and grain offerings, I will not accept them; and the offerings of well-being of your fatted animals I will not look upon. Take away from me the noise of your songs; I will not listen to the melody of your harps [Amos 5:21–23].

By itself, even worship—the hallmark of the religious life—is nothing, maybe worse than nothing. If this is the case, what could God possibly want? If worship and offering and praise are unacceptable, what is left? The prophet Amos continues and in doing so provides an answer: "But let justice roll down like waters, and righteousness like an ever-flowing stream" (Amos 5:24). The prophet, as he speaks the word from God, reveals that God speaks the word for the vulnerable. The prophet Micah puts it this way: "What does the LORD require of you but to do justice, and to love kindness, and to walk humbly with your God?" (Micah 6:8). If worship, if festivals and solemn assemblies, if offering and tithing, if hymns and praise and melodies are disconnected from justice, kindness, and humility, they are nothing. Worse, according to the prophets, God hates them. The religious life, apart from the righteousness and justice that watches out for those with little power, is a wolf in sheep's clothing. Manipulation preys on others. And the prophetic eye of faith, by being in touch with God's love of justice and concern for the vulnerable, is particularly sensitive to injustice, meanness, and the hubris of power.

For parents, the concern over manipulation has a double relevancy. First, children are in a vulnerable position relative to adults. The prophetic eye looks at us, as parents, condemning the ways we are tempted to manipulate those who are vulnerable in our care. Faith holds parents to greater vision. On the positive side, as we try to treat our own children with justice, humility, and kindness, they are learning to develop the vision as well. Second, as our children move into a larger world beyond their home and family life, they can become even more vulnerable to manipulative efforts. Children need the prophetic eye of a parent to watch out for them. Children need to learn to watch out for themselves as well.

One of the most difficult situations Jane and I have had to deal with as parents came when we discovered that the man who moved to our neighborhood, the man who came by frequently to chat, was on parole from jail for repeated offenses of pedophilia. The parole officer warned, "Don't let him anywhere near your children." Our children were only four and seven at the time. Fortunately, we had a history of talking fairly openly about our bodies, privacy, "good touch/bad touch," and selected rudiments of sexuality with our children. That helped. Nonetheless, the deeper difficulty was explaining to such young children the extent to which an adult could manipulate a relationship with a child. The difficulty was trying to explain how a physical intimacy that could be so wonderful and enjoyable in some contexts could be so terrible in others. We could almost see Adam and Eve in our children's eyes as they awakened to the tree of knowledge of good and evil.

THE COMPLEXITY OF SIN

Sin, from this perspective, is dynamic and complex. Our nature gives us powers and capacities, which themselves are good; they deepen life and love and relationships. But the open, free character of our nature allows us to mishandle our power to the harm of life, love, and our relationships. In reality, freedom, loving relationship, and creativity are all inter-related. Biblically, the power of the new *creation* is the power of *liberation* from death, is the power of God's *loving relationship*. But escapism, idolatry, and manipulation are inter-related as well. King David's *manipulations* were also a kind of *idolatry* (of his own power), which let him *escape* his responsibilities to those (the vulnerable) under his leadership.

Often trouble occurs through a hyperextension of one kind of good at the expense of others. An emphasis on freedom can lead to excessive individualism to the detriment of communities, congregations, families, parenting, and relationships generally. Yet an emphasis on relationships without regard for individual freedom can lead to other problems. Good relationships do not override individual dignity, respect, and honor born of freedom. A person may well need to get away from, to get out of, or to run from an awful situation. A person may need to flee. It would be irresponsible not to teach our children to run from the man trying to seduce them into a car or home. It would be cruel to advise a woman and her children to return to an abusive household. Faith wants people to see themselves as mysteries and treasure and protect their own lives accordingly.

The complex nature of sin reflects the complex nature of human existence. We are able to get close to others, get away from danger, create new possibilities, or make a mess of it all as well. The deep relationships of family life make us particularly vulnerable to one another, as well as responsible. Children are taking it all in. Long before they go to any school, they are learning how to be an individual and how to be part of a community at the same time. They are learning how vulnerability is treated. Maybe vulnerability evokes care and humility; maybe the vulnerable are bullied. The complexity of our natures contributes to the depth and meaning of human existence, but it contributes to the possibility of distortion as well. So the stakes are very high. Our ways of being family—what we value, whom we respect, what we allow, what we will never allow, how we talk to one another, how we touch one another, our dreams and hopes, our fears and concerns—all constitute the spiritual training of our children. Showing love and kindness to our children, teaching them to seek justice and to care for the vulnerable in society, letting them know that we, their parents, also bow before a God of mercy and goodness—these are the spiritual disciplines of parenting and the piety of home. Without them, as the prophets would remind us, our solemn prayers around the dinner table, our devotions, our scripture reading, our holidays, or our conversations about God are nothing, maybe worse than nothing.

The Insecurity of Life

So if sin is less about breaking rules and more about twisting the good things in life, why do we sin? What is the driving power behind sin itself? Why don't we all just stick to the good? So far, I have only described what this twisting looks like, but an even deeper question is, What makes sin so tempting? There are many theological schools of thought about this, but nearly all of them note the role that fear, mistrust, and insecurity play. And so often these are powerfully related to loss and death. In other words, I am suggesting that sin is deeply related to death, to the nothingness discussed in Genesis, to the void, to the dust. How so?

We all live under the constant threat of loss, harm, or even death. Some people certainly live with more threats and loss than others, but, nonetheless, no matter how much power or financial security or good health a person might have, life is still precarious. In the end is the end. We die. Kierkegaard called it *finitude*—the fact that life is finite, not infinite. We do not last. Life is inherently fragile. Death undermines all our freedoms, all our relationships, all our creations. Even if our own mortality does not bother us so much, perhaps worse, the mortality of friends and family members can be even more threatening. Not only am I vulnerably finite, so are the attachments of my heart. Things perish; people die. The very threads that hold us together are constantly fraying. Not only do we suffer losses but we know we ourselves lose in the end. That is, we remember past losses and anticipate future ones, including losing our own lives or the lives of those we love the most. Like a fault line running through existence, finitude makes the ground we live on very shaky indeed. Once we are old enough to realize our insecure situation, it is as if we have bitten from the forbidden tree. Paradise is lost. The situation makes for trouble.

So we are tempted—tempted to run away from commitments or relationships so as not to get hurt. Maybe if I don't get too attached, I won't be so hurt. Work, causes, and addictions are good places to hide. Scared, we run. Or maybe we hold on too tightly. Grab some security—maybe more insurance, more money, more education, or more religion. But there is never enough; there never could be enough to secure us in the face of the deepest threats. In family life, we might try to make our families do more than is possible. We can try to make them protect us from disappointment and loss, from our fears and insecurities. We can expect our spouses to be everything to us, to make us feel good all the time, to read our minds and calm our fears, to be the perfect lover, housekeeper, provider, friend, conversation partner, or parent. We can try to make them be gods for us. We can even expect any or all of these things of ourselves, as if perfection would somehow magically ward off our deepest sense of vulnerability. Yet the "perfect" life will still end in death.

With manipulation, too, fear is at work, even creating vicious circles. The more I might feel driven and bossed, the more I am tempted to gain control over others. The more I was jerked around at work today, the more angry I am that the house is a mess or my kids won't do what I asked them to do. The more out of control I feel, the more tempting it may be to control what I can, usually those in the most vulnerable position. A lot of family violence is born and perpetuated through such vicious circles. And a lot of more subtle damage to family relationships and communities occurs when there is such an atmosphere.

These are just some of the ways that the inherent insecurity of life tempts us in relation to home life. Much larger versions of such temptations can happen at greater scales. Whole nations can run (not care, become isolationist), promise salvation (through nationalism or an economic system), or manipulate (abuse citizens, attack other nations). All realms of human existence can be twisted through the sting of death, and this is the world in which children are trying to grow up.

———

Sin is a tough subject to take up. It haunts us with horrible things; it reminds us of our own personal failures and flaws and scares us, knowing how vulnerable our children are. Sin is deceptively complex. Running in one situation may be good; in another it is bad. Loving one thing is bad; loving another is good. Inevitably, however, as parents we have to deal with tough situations. Part of the power of faith is that faith has a long history of dealing with the most difficult situations of life: good and evil, power and vulnerability, sin and redemption, life and death. If this analysis of the role of fear and insecurity is accurate, faith is a constructive power if it can meet and address this fundamental fault line running through our lives.

Parenting by faith, raising our children in faith, learning the life of faith will involve cultivating the deepest sense of security—one that endures through life and death alike. Out of such security, temptation loses power.

Chapter 6

FROM FEAR TO COURAGE

Katherine Paterson's award-winning book *Bridge to Terabithia* is read in grade schools throughout the country. It is a beautiful story of friendship between two children, Jessie and Leslie, but it is also a story of loss. Unexpectedly, Leslie dies. Katherine Paterson says that many adults tell her that they have given the book to a child who has recently lost someone close. Her response to this is, "Too late." She explains, "The time to read *Bridge* is before they lose someone. Children need practice dealing with difficult issues, and stories can help them do so."

The biblical story of Israel and Christianity reveals the major role that loss, destruction, and oppression have played in the history of faith: floods, slavery, destroyed temples, homelessness, conquering nations, exile, and death. Yet over and over, the story also reveals how people of faith discover and rediscover deep sources of hope, courage, and new life. Covenants, blessings, the promised land, temples rebuilt, home, new life, love, new creation, and more. Hearing stories of struggle and redemption, whether in our families or in the family of faith, not only inspires but paves the way for our own ability to face loss and difficulty and discover sources of courage that endure. They are a gift to children.

SCARY DAYS

It is easy for adults to forget how scary the world can be to children, even when life seems to be going along fine. Simple changes or new places can evoke monsters at bedtime. Changing a routine, meeting new people, or getting a different babysitter can be quite intimidating to a child. Then when larger changes or more challenging situations arise, the ground can get very shaky for child or parent alike. New phases of life are often a particularly vulnerable time: having a new baby in the family, moving to a new town, starting or ending school. Families with children get a double dose of anxiety—a child's and a parent's.

We have a photograph of our oldest, David, boarding a massive school bus as he heads for his first day of kindergarten. The first step of the bus comes to his belly, and as he takes it, his knee comes to his chin. It would be like an adult trying to step onto the hood of a car. He is ready but nervous.

After the bus drove off, I rushed to a dental appointment, and in response to the dentist's innocent question, "How are you?" I began telling him all about watching my little-bitty boy get on the great big bus for the first time and how much more difficult it was to watch than I had anticipated. The dentist responded, "I know what you mean."

"Yeah, how so?"

He answered, "I just took my oldest kid to college for the first time yesterday. It doesn't get any easier."

For a parent, sending a child of any age off to school, especially a new school, can be unnerving. All these large issues of attachment and detachment, of holding on and letting go, come into sharp focus. For a child, fear has more to do with moving into the unknown. Parents, however, know too much. We want to shelter and protect our children on the one hand; on the other, we want them to grow up and thrive in the world. Negotiating the way can be tough business.

In her column in the journal *Family Ministry,* Wendy Wright tells of her youngest son's first day of high school. Before he left, she reached from behind and hugged and kissed the unsuspecting teenager. "'Mom!' he pleaded, half embarrassed, half annoyed by the intrusion." She reports, "I resumed a distance more conscious of the personal space needs of an emergent adolescent ego." At every age, parents and their offspring are negotiating how to be close, when to keep distance, how tight the cord should be, and how loose. At such transitional moments of our family lives—first days of school, for example—so much can be seen: a mother's love and affection, a youngest son's growing up. When the ride to school came for Wendy Wright's son, "He opened the door then uncharacteristically twisted back around, searching the room to see if I was there. He seemed relieved that I was. 'Bye,' he gestured awkwardly. 'Have a great day,' I smiled. Then with a click of the door latch he was gone."

Getting close, backing off, affection, annoyance, hugs, kisses, gestures, words, smiles, assurances, goodbyes—this is the everyday substance of human relationships. This is the everyday substance of love itself. As Wendy Wright puts it, "The moments are at once so terribly mundane and so transparently sacred; ordinary moments which, for an instant, connect us to the depth, width, height and length of love. Family life is full of them." We need that kind of love to thrive. We need the tangible reminders of this love that close relationships can provide.

But what happens when those reminders themselves are not as solid as we may have believed? When we sent David to school for the first time, we were beginning our fifth year in Princeton, New Jersey, and living in a student housing complex with other families who had come from all parts of this country and the world to be in seminary. Our son was just one among many of these little five-year-olds riding the humongous yellow school bus. No parents were allowed—an actual rule. David, despite his parents' anxiety, actually handled it pretty well. It helped tremendously that he knew other kids on the bus and that he knew other kids at school from our housing complex. The town itself was familiar to him; it was the only place he could remember. And Mom and Dad and sister Cora were still there when he got home. All that helped.

One of the other kindergarten children on the bus was Ben. Ben's family had just moved into our complex a few days before

From Fear to Courage

school began. To David's delight, there was Ben, who was also five years old and would also be starting school. David and Ben hit it off immediately. Ben had come all the way from the West Coast, from Los Angeles. His parents had just gotten a divorce. And now Ben had to start all-day kindergarten and ride the big yellow school bus and come home to a strange little apartment to half his parents. It was a shaky time.

In spite of these challenges, Ben found the courage to ride the bus and went to school that first day. When he got home in the afternoon, his mother, concerned, asked him how it went. Ben said, "Well Mom, I got scared a few times, but then I would just look over and see David's head and I knew everything would be okay."

Who could imagine that a young friendship could be so powerful? In this case, David was both the familiar face of a friend and a connection to his new home. The combination of friendship and the reminder of home went a long way toward allowing Ben to get through an anxious day in an overwhelming world. Children may scare easily, but they are creative and resourceful as well.

COURAGE FOR LIFE

These situations tell us a lot about the courage needed in life, even needed by little children or adolescents as they circle into a larger world. Parents need it, too, especially as they risk sending their children into this larger world and new realms. Courage, as many insightful thinkers have pointed out, is not so much the absence of fear but the power to act wisely in the midst of fear. Courage is the power to live in spite of insecurity. Courage does not eliminate threat. It reaches for something deeper than the threat. So whether it is a child going to school or Moses facing the Pharaoh, courage to live and thrive in the face of threats is needed in dramatic and ordinary situations alike.

For our son, David, the following year, starting first grade was a very different story for him. This time, we were the new people, having just moved to Oshkosh, Wisconsin. We moved to town in the

THE POWER OF GOD AT HOME

summer and spent two months in a rental; then that house was sold out from under us, and we had to move again. We found a new home as school was starting, so David began first grade at the school in the neighborhood we were moving into. Consequently, there was not even one face at school familiar to him—not a soul.

Even so, our son managed pretty well that first day. He managed pretty well the second day, too. The third day was the day we moved into our new home. And that morning David was having a terrible time getting his shoes on before school.

"Dad, my feet hurt." So I tried to help him get his shoes on. But it didn't work. The socks were too lumpy; there was a rough seam in the sneaker; his toe was sore. Finally, in tears, David revealed, "You know sometimes your feet hurt when you are homesick." We got assurance that this would not be a habit and let David stay home "helping us move" all that day, barefoot. In fact, he wouldn't leave my side for anything. I was pretty nervous about this. I had visions of trying to talk a thirty-year-old David into putting his shoes on.

That afternoon the doorbell rang. I answered and it was Joey, another six-year-old from David's class who lived a few doors away from our new place. He asked, "Can David come to my house and play?" I started to make an excuse for the child, still half-hidden behind my leg, when David shot out the door. And the next morning, knowing he had a friend at school, David's feet felt better. Who would have guessed a young friendship could be so powerful? In this case, Joey had become the familiar face—the face that would bridge home and school, the face that generated courage in an overwhelming world.

Parents live in a multi-tiered world. As adults, they may be dealing with large-scale issues at work or in the community. They may be wrestling with global concerns or national problems. At the same time, they may be trying to put a child's shoes on or calm a nightmare. Yet whatever the tier, issues of fear and courage, insecurity and comfort pervade worlds large and small alike. Adults know that nightmares come and nightmares go, but to the child the nightmare may be everything. Children need concrete assurances that the nightmare is not reality, that hurting feet will feel better, or that everything's going to be okay. Often these assurances come in the form of people—

From Fear to Courage

a parent, a friend, a familiar face. Attached to others who care, the child's world gets bigger than the nightmare. A hug is hope; play empowers. If this is true on a smaller scale, perhaps it is true on larger ones as well.

The Securing Power of Faith

In Chapter Five I suggested that the fear and insecurity generated by the fragile, finite nature of existence play a large role in twisting the good things of life into destructive ones. Instead of freedom, love, and creativity, the result is escape, idolatry, and manipulation. In a sense, death (loss, nothingness, the formless void) co-opts the good for its own demonic purposes. By this logic and in contrast, however, courage and security play a large role in untwisting the twisted. Or perhaps courage and security make temptations less tempting in the first place. If this were true, courage and security would be real power over the demons of death.

I believe this is, in fact, the power of faith. The Creator of life is a solid security in the midst of shaky ground. "O LORD, my rock and my redeemer" is how Psalm 19 puts it. God's power to redeem is tied to knowing God as a rock that is solid beneath our feet. This is eternal security that endures through death itself. How important and reassuring such security can be for those facing death and loss. Death is not the last word. Even death cannot separate us from the love of God, says Paul. Yet a major point would be lost if this redemption were limited only to the afterlife. Deep security—God's love—breeds good things here and now. The more we can rest assured in God's love, the more we know and live by grace, the more death loses its sting in our lives. And I believe this is the deepest kind of empowerment for family life. I believe this is the deepest kind of spiritual training for children. God's securing love redeems life because it helps us loosen our grip on idols. It helps us come out of hiding. The love of God is the power to resist manipulation.

So faith is a matter of recognizing God's redeeming relationship to humanity—a relationship of lifegiving love that is already there before we have done or thought or believed anything at all. But to recognize this love, we have to see through the dark glass of finitude and into the abundance of life that death cannot conquer. Spiritual education involves cultivating the eyes to see abundance, to attend to mystery, and to perceive everlasting love in order to know, as Paul puts it, "even as I have been fully known."

Perhaps now it is clearer why faith puts us in touch with such a large view of the world. It is for a reason: it helps us see and know and live by the securing power of infinite love. We are being stretched toward eternity. The story of faith stretches our minds and imaginations so far back, to the beginning, and so far forward, to the end and beyond. Our identities stretch beyond our individual egos or beyond our own family trees to the family of faith. Our vision expands to see in depth, to recognize the holiness of others. Faith not only stretches our minds and identities and vision but faith stretches our hearts to find a secure home. Kierkegaard said that in faith, "the self rests transparently in the power that established it." Threats and loss do not go away, but, by faith, threats and loss do not define existence. Reality is larger than the nightmare. As the Apostle Paul put it, "Where, O death, is your victory? Where, O death, is your sting?" (1 Corinthians 15:55). Faith recognizes the wider, deeper context of life. Faith knows that the creative power that could bring flesh to the valley of dry bones, that could bring the Israelites home, that could raise the crucified body of Jesus, that can transform heaven and earth into a home where God and mortals can dwell together—faith knows that this power is ultimate. This is the power that establishes us. Escape, idolatry, and manipulation are cheap imitations of power that will fade away into nothingness. God will "wipe every tear from their eyes," says the Book of Revelation. "Death will be no more; mourning and crying and pain will be no more" (21:4). This is a glimpse of a whole larger than the threatening parts. Everything will be okay.

CARING COMMUNITIES

The kind of courage rooted in faith is not something we can just muster up by sheer willpower. Our willpower simply is not great enough to take on death and loss. We lose. Instead, the kind of courage born of faith is a gift. It comes from beyond us, but it comes to us. At best we can keep our eyes open, listen for its rhythms, and rest secure.

Even so, rest itself is often disturbed. Parts of life will continue to threaten. And because this is so, because our glimpses into security are themselves only peeks (and colored by insecurity at that), we need constant and concrete reminders of the love that cares for us ultimately. People are crucial. An important way in which we come to know a care larger than ourselves is to experience it through others and offer it to them as well. Caring communities, by faith, give courage. Families and congregations alike are in a good position to be caring communities (they are both full of people). Attached to those who care, our vision of things gets clearer. The image of God in others reflects God to us.

The writer and novelist Anne Lamott has written a brutally honest, often irreverent but nonetheless profound account of her son's first year of life and her first year as a parent. The book is titled *Operating Instructions*. Lamott admits she is intensely neurotic; she is a recovering alcoholic, a single mother, and, to top it all off, a committed Christian (with a mouth like a sailor). She sugarcoats nothing, including what it is like to be a new mom trying to go it alone, admitting how indescribably exhausted she has become.

She writes under the journal entry for October 13, "Last night I decided that it is totally nuts to believe in Christian. . . . Then something truly amazing happened."

A man from her church had showed up at her home; it was her associate pastor's husband. He said to her, "Margaret and I wanted to do something for you and the baby. So what I want to ask is, What if a fairy appeared on your doorstep and said that he or she would do any favor for you at all, anything you wanted around the house that you felt too exhausted to do by yourself and too ashamed to ask anyone else to help you with?"

"I can't even say; it's too horrible."

He insisted and finally persuaded her. She said that it would be to clean the bathroom, and "he ended up spending an hour scrubbing the bathtub and toilet and sink with Ajax and lots of hot water." She reports that she sat on the couch watching TV, feeling vaguely guilty and nursing her son Sam to sleep. "But it made me feel sure of Christ again, of that kind of love. This, a man scrubbing a new mother's bathtub, is what Jesus means to me."

The securing power of faith releases care and community, yet care and community offer security. Made in the image of God, we are made to love, so each act of care reflects the Holy One's passion for life. Even the humblest act flowing from such a source takes on meaning that is radically amazing. "The divine sings in our good deeds," says Abraham Heschel; "the divine is disclosed in our sacred deeds." Mitzvot, or sacred deeds, are "points of eternity in the flux of temporality." As the eternal is glimpsed, so is eternal security, even through the act of cleaning a bathroom. From this point of view, the divine sings through the simple acts of care.

Caring deeds are some of the good fruits of life in the Spirit of God. Sometimes we are the caregivers; sometimes we are the vulnerable ones in need of tender hands. Family life is fertile soil for learning about care and vulnerability; patterns of life and mind alike are being established for children there. Either directly or indirectly, families constantly provide answers to such questions as, Who is lovable? Am I? Are others in my family? Are the rules different for some than others? How about those outside my family? Who should I care for? Much of the time, the answers to such questions are answered tacitly through attitudes and actions, but, nonetheless, children are soaking them in. Children are continually learning how to see themselves and how to see others. When Robert Coles asked Ruby Bridges why she was praying for those people who were yelling such angry things at her, the little girl responded, "Well, don't you think those people need praying for?"

From Fear to Courage

The story of Ruby Bridges going to school (see Chapter One) highlights an important warning when it comes to the role of communities in faith. The spirit of a community matters. Tragically, whole communities can form more out of fear and insecurity and twist care into "caring just for our own kind" or twist community into a self-enclosed cult or an angry mob. That is why the message of a community matters, why its character is important, and why the concrete practices of a community are crucial. They reveal how big or small the community's view of the world is; they reveal how large or small its circle of concern is. Ultimately, the message, character, and practices of a community reveal how secure it is, or how insecure. Do the messages taught and affirmed in this congregation narrow thinking or stretch it? Do practices in this family generate loving care or hateful scapegoating? Over time, does this community empower people or drain them? Of course, these are always a matter of degree. No community is perfect; even the best will have its failures. But the ability to recognize failures and flaws is also an important mark of security for a community. That is, is the community solid enough to face its own sin? Can it be self-critical as a community, not just as individuals? Does it have ways of making amends? Or is the community hopelessly stuck in its ways, even when they hurt?

In all communities (families and congregations alike), care is crucial to reflecting the securing power of God's eternal love to people, but to do so, the whole group cannot override the individual dignity of its members. Good community enhances individuality and vice versa. As Paul Tillich's *The Courage to Be* puts it, faith generates the "courage to be as a part" and it generates the "courage to be as oneself."

Just as communities enrich individual lives, individual lives enrich communities. Neither parts (individuals) nor the whole (community) can offer the full picture. In marriage, for example, individual lives join to form a new community. Shared love, common experiences, mutual respect, and responsibility all enrich the lives of each individual. Yet the individual experiences of each—coming from their personalities, interests, and talents, their families of origin and old friendships—enrich the relationship itself. So do children. In families, if an individual dominates in one way or another, the individuality of the others easily gets lost to the detriment of the family as a whole. Letting members be individuals can be difficult, and it is particularly difficult for parents. Because parents carry the larger burden of responsibility in a family with children (especially the younger or more vulnerable the children are), it is easy for parents to override a child's own thoughts, feelings, gifts, tastes, and talents with their own. Although there is a hierarchy of responsibility (parent over child), there does not have to be a hierarchy of personality or individuality. However, it is no better for a child to overrun parents either. A child is strengthened in his or her individuality by feeling deeply a part of a family. Children have to learn how to live with and respect others as well. Individuality can feed family life; family life can feed individuality.

The Song of Creation

The fact is that this relationship between individuals and community is not only a feature of human relationship but is a feature of life itself. The picture gets bigger. All living systems need this interplay between part and whole to thrive. The body of an elephant as well as the human body needs the integrity of its individual organs (parts) to live, but the organs work together, creating so much more than the sum of the parts. The heart alone will die if not working within a larger system of the body. The body will die without the heart. Communities and families are similar; its members struggle and wither without a larger context of love and security. Families and communities struggle and wither when their members are cut off from the whole.

The lively interplay between part and whole happens at all levels of creation. Atoms are composed of systems of subatomic particles; atoms themselves compose larger layers of reality. Galaxies are composed of stars and their universes; galaxies themselves compose an even larger cosmos. Similarly, households are composed of individual members, while households themselves constitute larger communities.

Every level of life, whether a body or a galaxy, has its own crucial integrity, even while each level opens onto even larger contexts. In the case of families, they risk withering if they cut themselves off from larger levels of community, such as neighborhoods, congregations, civic life, or the larger society in general. However, these larger communities wither without the integrity of families contributing to the whole. For example, a society's deep suspicion of families is no better than a family's deep suspicion of a society. (Again, families and communities such as intensely abusive families, cults, and totalitarian regimes may warrant suspicion, but these too have been twisted by that devil, fear. A sure sign of their bedevilment is their use of fear itself as a weapon.) The larger point is that part and whole need each other; where they work together, whether at the level of galaxies, families, congregations, or subatomic particles, there is life.

The first chapter of Genesis illustrates the theological significance of the interplay between part and whole. God speaks creation into existence. For example, "God said, 'Let there be light'; and there was light" (3). Jürgen Moltmann notes that, as God speaks life into being, Genesis reveals the character of creative life. God's speech, like human speech, involves individual words as well as breath. "The word names, differentiates and appraises. But the breath is the same in all the words, and binds the words together." Words differentiate; the breath binds. As Moltmann puts it, the Creator differentiates life through the Word of God but joins life in the Spirit. The implication is that the interplay between differentiated parts and a binding whole reflects God's creative speech. The implication for family life is that all the struggles and challenges involved in letting each other be individuals while trying to be a community at the same time, all the struggles to be different and to stick together at the same time, all the struggles of letting our children pursue their gifts and personal interests while making sure we have time together as a family—these are not only matters of family functioning but they are theological struggles. The good is at stake.

According to Moltmann, creation is more than speech; creation is a song. "In the quickening breath and through the form-giving word, the Creator sings out his creatures in the sounds and rhythms in which he has his joy and his good pleasure." The interplay between part and whole reflects the hymn at the heart of creation.

CREATIVE LIVING

The previous chapter noted the interconnection between freedom, loving relationship, and creativity rooted in the image of God in humanity. Here we can observe that when parts and whole are working well together, creative possibilities emerge, maybe even a song or two. Untwisted, freedom generates individual dignity; love generates community care, and creativity generates life. Can you hear the music?

Creativity is the power to work with the stuff of our lives in fruitful ways. Creativity, in this sense, is not simply tied to fine arts or crafts, though it may include them; it is more about living. It could include the power to create or recreate a family by getting married or adopting a child or giving birth, for example. It can involve creating play, games, rituals, plans, vacations, trips, projects, or even rest. It can be creating a meal, which in turn may be creating time together, good company, nourishment, and enjoyment. As the temptation to manipulate others softens, as resistance to the manipulations of others strengthens, creativity is the power that allows us to create our own lives and see the beauty of others.

The power to create life—literally, culturally, artistically, playfully—is crucial to a community's integrity. A family, like an individual, needs a sense that it is in control of its own life. That means making choices, living out its own values, and having time of its own. To the extent that families can make choices, live out its own values, and have time together, they discover profound sources of meaning and dignity. But the more these signs of creative life are threatened or undermined, the more difficult it is to sustain family life. In totalitarian states, the threats to creativity and family life alike come from the government. Family power threatens state power. Why? Because robust family life generates resistance to manipulation. In a similar vein, it is no accident that American slavery constantly broke families apart.

But freer societies generate their own kind of threats to family life, their own ways in which they are hard on creative living. For example, in a consumer-driven economy, manipulation is more subtle than a government crack-down on free speech, but its subtlety makes it more difficult to see. Increasingly, we are tempted to hand creative living over to the god of consumption. The goal of most advertising is to manipulate our sensibilities into thinking we need to consume this product or service to be happy. From entertainment to hygiene, from transportation to food, you need what they have—now. Hurry! Call this number! The quicker we can be driven to this madness, the harder it is to resist. And when the bill comes, it's time to put in more hours at work, which only drives us more. The point is that the more others (with less than noble motives) create our lives for us and run our daily patterns, the less meaningful our lives and daily patterns are.

The creative life, however, sees alternatives. Creative family life has a larger vision, allowing for new possibilities. While consumerism may say, "Spend more to find happiness," creative courage may answer, "We are happy to spend time together." While the entertainment industry may blare out, "Buy the latest CD," creative living may reply, "We'll sing our own music tonight." As the Sunday paper screams, "Biggest Sale Of The Year, Today Only," creative rest may whisper, "Let's lie low today." Or when the latest book promises, "Here's how to be the perfect family," creative love replies, "We will live by grace."

The more that larger communities, such as congregations, can encourage, honor, and respect such creativity in its families, the better. The more that parents can encourage, honor, and respect such creativity with their children, the better. It is not always easy. Congregations and parents alike usually have large agendas with too little time. But as David Elkind put it many years ago in his book *The Hurried Child*, it is easy to "hurry" our children right through childhood. Nine times out of ten, hurrying is the bad fruit of some kind of manipulation, and it certainly is a killer of creativity. Whether it is because a child is running late because she was glued to the television or he is rushing from one activity to the next, the child's life is slipping away. Creativity cannot be hurried. It flourishes by the rhythms of activity and rest alike. It needs time to work and time to play. Creativity needs time, period.

Biblically, time itself is more a creative act than a measurable quantity. In Genesis, the beginning of time ("in the beginning") coincides with creation and occurs before there is even a sun or moon to measure time. For God, Sarah's measurable age is irrelevant to her capacity to give birth. Biblically, time is fertile, open to creative possibilities—generations and generations of them. The implication is that the collapse of time (hurrying) coincides with a collapse of creative power, which is a symptom of manipulation.

Of course there will be times or phases of family life that are incredibly complex; schedules must be juggled (the teen years come to mind). This can be a sign of children growing up, developing their interests and activities, and generally creating their own lives. But that same creativity can be employed by families to "make time" in the midst of hectic schedules. Meals together, a drive or walk, reading a book out loud, or playing a game, for example, can do wonders for creating a sense of dignity and delight in a family (even with teenagers).

Even so, creative living involves more than making time and resisting manipulation. In faith, creativity serves love and tends care as well, sustaining them with joy and beauty. The kind of joy and beauty, bred by faith, is not always obvious in our cosmetic-surgery culture, but it may be there all the same. I have learned much about this from my own children.

One day a few years ago, as I walked into the room I got ticked. I had told them to clean up, but as I came down the stairs I could see more and more mess. Layers of cloth and fabric were strewn all over; there were threads, baskets, beads, scissors, old clothes, buttons, and more. The room was a disaster and in the eye of the storm was Cora, sewing away. Then, as I looked across the room, I realized it was worse. Half-opened packages of modeling clay were everywhere; some of the clay was ground into the floor. Paints, brushes, magazines, and cans were all over, with my clay-smeared son in the middle of it all. I yelled something about disrespecting the house and disrespecting me and wanting some answers and who knows what and then stared at them like a mean cat, waiting to pounce on their inadequate excuses.

Knowing the look, Cora said, "I'm done. I'll clean up."

"Me too," David followed. "I already started," he said, trying to win me over a little.

"You have thirty minutes."

Thirty-three minutes later, they came bounding upstairs: "Wanna see, wanna see?" I looked; it was marginally adequate and I said so.

"What do you think?"

"I said it was clean enough, though you missed here."

"No," said Cora, "What do you think of the bag?" She held up the bag she had hand-sewn as a gift to a friend at church—not a birthday present or anything else, just a gift.

"And the flower," followed David. He held up an intricate little flower pot, no more than an inch and a half tall, sculpted from the clay, with a delicate flower he had also made poking out the top. "It's for MeMe!" (their great-grandmother, whom I was going to visit in the hospital). "It should last longer than a regular flower."

"They're beautiful," I finally answered. And though David and Cora weren't totally sure why, I found myself apologizing to them.

Despite their father's impatience, Cora and David managed a couple of creative acts of friendship and care. Children will often do that if they are given half a chance. This is territory where adults can learn a lot from children, if we pay attention. (Do not get me wrong; children can act mean and nasty, too. But scratch beneath the surface, and you will probably discover a lot of fear lurking near the nastier places in their hearts.) Before children are led to believe that buying is better than creating, they love to make things and give them away. One of my dresser drawers is stuffed with poems, homemade cards, drawings, collages, and the like that I cannot bear to throw away. They are expressions of love.

SECURING SECURITY

Security is power because it releases life. Security releases freedom and, with it, dignity, self-respect, and individual gifts. Security releases communion and, with it, friendships, community, and care. Security releases creativity as well and, with it, possibilities, new life, and beauty. These are signs of courage. These are sources of the good. This puts the everyday deeds of parenting in a theological perspective. Even the simplest household acts mean more than we can say. Hugging a child after a nightmare, wiping a tear, holding a hand. With each comforting touch, a child feels the River of Life flowing. Playing catch, going for a walk, sitting on a porch visiting— children are learning a power over anxious hurrying. Part of us may wish that the Sunday or Hebrew school would take care of our children's religious training, but no classroom can pull off this kind of learning. For these reasons and more, parenting is more meaningful than we can say.

Even so, parents are not perfect; even if we were, perfection cannot endure forever because we do not endure forever. Even the securing power of a parent is still subject to a fragile life. At some point, children learn that the foundation laid by their loving, securing parents is itself shaky, not infinite. Not only failure but loss through illness, separation, and death reveals a fault line. This means that our children are well served if they can learn to know an ultimate security that sustains and motivates the partial securities they have known. Once again, the relationship between part and whole is crucial. Without the parts—without the particular concrete experiences of love, care, comfort, and freedom—the whole is empty and makes no sense. But without a sense of the whole—a sense that there is a love more enduring than the fragile love known in part—the everyday experiences of love lose power.

The genius of faith lies in its paradoxical affirmation. God transcends this universe; God is also present to it. This is key. For in this paradox, God is a security that is not finite, not subject to what the Apostle Paul calls the "futility." Yet this infinite God is not so grand or distant as to be remote from human beings. This is not Isaac Newton's watchmaker God, winding up the universe like a clock and letting it go. Through the Spirit, God is present, infusing life with the power of love. Paul says this in his letter to the Romans: "For I am convinced that neither death, nor life, nor angels, nor rulers, nor things present, nor things to come, nor powers, nor height, nor depth, nor anything else in all creation, will be able to separate us from the love of God in Christ Jesus our Lord" (8:38–39).

In Christian communities, this is a favorite passage for memorial and burial services. It points to a reality larger than the terrible loss that loved ones are going through. And the passage reveals the character of that larger reality—a love that will not let us go. This love is freeing. It is the opposite of bondage. "You did not receive a spirit of slavery to fall back into fear," says Paul, "but you have received a spirit of adoption." Although life and its inevitable losses may leave us feeling like frightened orphans at times, the conviction here is that we are adopted, that the Spirit gathers us in to be "children of God" (12:15–16).

No matter how together, well managed, effective, highly functioning, or even securing our family lives may be, they are ever fragile. Without a Security that remains beneath the everyday securities, without a Spirit that rests beneath our family spirit, without a Love that endures beyond the finite loves a household can offer, there is an underlying sense of futility. Futility drains the joy, meaning, and power right out of life. Yet the vision of faith sees a larger picture. The Spirit of God undergirds everyday securities, family spirit, and household love in ways that set life free. Rather than a sense of futility, everyday family living, in this Spirit, can make the larger picture visible. Like bread or wine, like manna or a candle, something ordinary and visible can reveal what is extraordinary and invisible. Maybe hugs and assuring words—maybe a smile or a homemade gift can, too.

Chapter 7

WHAT'S IN
A HOME?

One of my hopes in writing this book is that, through it, those raising children can see how much they are already doing to till spiritual soil. My worry is that parents don't see it. And not seeing the deeper reality of what they are doing makes it easier to feel inadequate. Parents are not seeing themselves as spiritual teachers because they think teaching happens in classrooms and spirituality happens at synagogue or church. Spiritual teaching, by this logic, happens in religious classrooms. But if parents can see their home lives as spiritual territory, perhaps it will be easier to recognize how much teaching and learning happens there, and they can build on this knowledge.

So at this point, having explored the spiritual context of life itself through the Bible and theological themes, I would like to look again at homes and families and their meaning for the life of faith. As you will see, I think congregational life is critical to faith as well, so the chapter explores the relationship between homes and congregations. Along the way, I share a couple of exercises that I often do in my classes or with groups of parents. (If you are reading this book as part of a group, the group may want to try them; if you are reading on your own, they can still be meaningful for reflecting on home and family life.)

DEFINING TERMS

What exactly is a home? What is a family? Year after year, I have asked students and groups of parents to try to define these terms. Most find it more difficult than they thought it would be. Go ahead and try the exercise if you like.

A home is _____

A family is _____

Even when people settle on a definition, they often find they are not totally satisfied with it. I confess that I make it worse by asking, "What do you *not* like about your own definition?" Try this too if you want.

My definition of home did not include _____
_____

My definition of family forgot about _____
_____

So someone might say, "Home is the place I live" but then say, "My definition doesn't include my parents' home, which is still home to me in one way, or my home town, or the stuff in my apartment, which makes my place here home." Or someone might say, "A family consists of people related to each other by blood or marriage" but then say, "My roommates and I are like sisters; actually we are closer than my sisters and I are, and I would have to call them family." Or I have heard, "My definition left out pets; you cannot appreciate my family without knowing our dog." Or "I can't figure out where an ex-spouse would fit in. Legally my ex-husband is no longer my family, but because we share custody, I see him daily. And he is certainly my children's family."

Occasionally, a conscientious student will come up with a very formal, accurate, inclusive definition. Then the dissatisfaction goes something like this: "I can't think of anything that isn't family or home, and that doesn't seem right either" or "My definitions are pretty good intellectually, but they also strike me as incredibly boring" or "My definitions don't reflect what my home and family really mean to me. What's a definition without meaning?" And so it goes.

In class, the exercise is intended to initiate a conversation about the mystery of home and families; there is a fullness to these realities that frustrates our ability to capture them in words. But the same could be said for realities like love, or freedom, or friendship, or God. The reality of family or home is more fluid than definitions tend to allow, not to mention more emotionally loaded, yet all this is part of their meaning. In other words, the difficulty felt when trying to define family or home is a sign of their irreducibility, a clue to their mystery.

More productive, in terms of getting at meaning, has been asking people to tell a story about what family means to them—what home means. Or asking, "What are some of the more meaningful experiences in your home and family life?" This can be a very powerful exercise in group discussions, especially among parents. But if you try this in a group yourself, allow lots of time or give people a chance to tell and hear from at least one other person. Because once people think of a meaningful story, they need to tell it. Often the stories people tell or the experiences they share are not light, happy ones. In fact, sometimes the reflections are very painful; they hope to create a different kind of home, a different way of being a parent or spouse. These experiences, too, can be powerful to share in communities of care. And all these kinds of discussions can be helpful, not only in classroom settings but at home itself, among parents, or even with children (but be prepared for anything).

If the mood is right in a group—a little playful—I sometimes ask, "If you were creating a recipe for family (or home), what would the ingredients be?" I admit that this one is hokey, but it often reveals what people believe is most important about home and family life. Sometimes the stories people tell are very dramatic; sometimes the ingredients are profound. Just as often, though, the ingredients or stories involve very ordinary activities and elements: hugs and walks, daily routines, meals and ball games, or bedtime stories.

Claiming home life as spiritual territory is easier if you can see and feel its fullness. Spiritual things are hard to contain. This may challenge our ability to define them, but what a meager, bland world it would be if we could capture it all with words. Even the Bible's portrayal of home and family life resists easy characterization. If we look to the ancient households of the Bible, we discover some of the same challenges. Not only are they difficult to define, they shift. Biblically, for example, in one era a family might easily be polygamous; in another it may be monogamous. For this reason, I find myself wary of claims to a "biblical model of family." The Bible does give us clues, however, about the character of human relationships, including family relationships and what is essential in them. One of the most beautiful expressions comes from the Apostle Paul:

> If I speak in the tongues of mortals and of angels, but do not have love, I am a noisy gong or a clanging cymbal. And if I have prophetic powers, and understand all mysteries and all knowledge, and if I have all faith, so as to remove mountains, but do not have love, I am nothing. If I give away all my possessions, and if I hand over my body so that I may boast, but do not have love, I gain nothing [1 Corinthians 13:1–4].

Paul, the itinerant bachelor, gives families some of the greatest advice possible. Without love, the other things are irrelevant. They serve nothing. It all returns to nothingness except love.

Okay, but "love" is also one of those realities that is difficult to define, so where does that get us? Paul's way to describe love is this:

> Love is patient; love is kind; love is not envious or boastful or arrogant or rude. It does not insist on its own way; it is not irritable or resentful; it does not rejoice in wrongdoing, but rejoices in the truth. It bears all things, believes all things, hopes all things, endures all things. Love never ends [5–8].

If our homes and families are to be defined in light of Paul's words, we could say they are to be defined by love. However

Paul's words were not written for a particular family but for a whole community—an early Christian congregation in the town of Corinth. So not only is this wisdom for household life, it is wisdom for congregational living as well. As the following section explores, the line between the two—between congregation and home—was not so sharp as the contemporary mind tends to imagine.

GLIMPSING ANCIENT HOUSEHOLDS

In ancient Israel and early Judaism (roughly the period from the Exodus to the first century), the "family household" was the closest thing to what demographers might now call the "family unit." Beyond the household, larger extensions of family (tribes and clans) were important, too, but the household would have been the most intense expression of kinship itself. Yet these family households were typically very different from the contemporary notion of family units. They would certainly befuddle a U.S. census taker. As biblical scholar Leo Perdue explains, these households were "multigenerational (up to four generations) and included the social arrangement of several families, related by blood and marriage, who lived in two or three houses architecturally connected." Such a household typically would have included widows, servants, orphans, sojourners, workers, and even priests tending the family shrine. And not only people but the estate itself was part of the household—the fields, orchards, livestock, or vineyards, for example. These were critical to the household's survival. In an arrangement that would be startling to the modern imagination, the household would have also included not only the living but the dead as well—ancestors "who were remembered through story and ritual and, in some sense, continued to live through their descendants," as Perdue explains. The dead were buried on the household's land so they could continue as family members. In other words, the biblical notion of being gathered to or going to "the ancestors" had a quite literal dimension, as members of the household were buried in the family cemetery.

In all, the household included "the dead ancestors of the past, those living in the present, and those yet to be born." It is easy, then, to see how anemic the contemporary nuclear family would seem to these ancestors. (It is also easier to appreciate what was at stake, to the ancient mind, when Genesis declared that "Sarai was barren, she had no child.") The ancient household would have generated much of its own work, play, community, shelter, religion, education, and affection. In addition, a household could endure for generations.

The households of early Christianity also shake our imaginations, compared to contemporary home life. Houses did not separate public and private life in any manner even approaching the way we, in American society, imagine. In a typical Roman house, as New Testament scholars Carolyn Oseik and David Balch describe, anyone could enter the vestibule or atrium of a household, reserving private space only for dining rooms, bedrooms, and baths. "Access was much more fluid than modern persons typically allow, more analogous to modern businesses where customers regularly enter and leave than to modern Western homes." In other words, home life itself was more public than typical homes today. As is the case when talking about contemporary homes, these generalizations about ancient households do not capture the varieties and exceptions to the rule, but they tell us enough to reveal some important differences between contemporary families and households and ancient ones.

There is another factor of the first century that intensifies the importance of households in relation to religion. Recall that this century witnessed the destruction of the temple. This made households even more critical. When the temple was destroyed in the sixth century, in conjunction with the Babylonian exile, sustaining the religious life through household practice became critical to religious survival. The first century was similar. As the center of worship collapsed, household worship became crucial. Judaism particularly, through the centuries, has seen many more hard times and persecution; Judaism has been persecuted as a religion, and over and again household practice has been essential to hope as well as survival. In early Christianity (or churches), the household was decisive as well; these households *were* the churches. The Apostle Paul established these "ekklesiai" (Greek for "assemblies") in places like Corinth and Ephesus and many other cities throughout Asia Minor; the assemblies met in households for worship and meals. Rather than design new structures for these assemblies, Oseik and Balch explain, for possibly the first century and a half, these groups adapted themselves to the available structures. When groups became too large for the space, another "church" was founded elsewhere.

Given such domestic origins, it is probably no accident that "family" language became so important to churches. Throughout his letters to these assemblies (known in the New Testament as 1st and 2nd Corinthians or Ephesians), Paul repeatedly calls these people brothers and sisters. He does not address them as assembly members, church folk, righteous people, or even Christians. For Paul, life in the Spirit is life with others as brothers and sisters. It is a life of love and kindness and patience. It is a life where the gifts of each contribute to a common welfare—where money and food are distributed to any who have need, not just to the hardest-working family members. And as the parables of Jesus were remembered, the God of these household assemblies is like the father who runs with open arms to the lost son, like the woman who sweeps the house until she finds the lost coin. *Home* powerfully shaped the religious imagination and practice of early Christianity.

RELATING HOME AND CONGREGATION

The shaping was not one-way, however. The fluid boundaries between home life and religious life affected each realm, transforming both. On the one hand, the worshiping assembly is more like a household with brothers and sisters and meals and a shared life. On the other, households are more like worshiping assemblies, like temples—places of prayer and praise and study. This has an important and, I believe, helpful effect for our contemporary imaginations about congregational ministry in relation to families. As one local pastor where I live described their approach to family ministry, "The goal is to make church more like home and to make home

What's in a Home?

more like church." This kind of goal can help keep the mutually beneficially relationship between homes and congregations strong and ward off some of the dangers when the relationship is weak or domineering.

Families that try to keep their religion to themselves and practice it alone tend to be isolated and lose the wisdom and gifts of a larger community. Isolationism is typically rooted in fear, and breeds more fear. Families can become like little spiritual cults when they close themselves off from a larger community. It does not have to be a cult of bizarre religious rituals either; it can simply be the cult of nothing, plaguing its children with emptiness.

In the ancient world, the danger of large kinship systems and households was that they could close in and be oppressive for their members and hostile to neighbors and strangers. This is likely the kind of thing Jesus was addressing when he spoke of family relationships. When Jesus says, "Whoever does the will of my Father in heaven is my brother and sister and mother," he not only widens the circle but he, in one line, transforms an understanding of both family and religious community. He takes literal relationships and uses them to describe community relationships. He uses community relationships to free up family relationships.

But the larger context of community life has its own dangers. Congregations, for example, can actually pull families apart in the name of God. This can happen directly and dramatically in spiritual cults, for example, which typically sever family ties. But more often than not, such coercion happens subtly through a surfeit of programs and meetings and services that regularly divide families up. Ironically, this danger can be the greatest in larger, busier congregations that offer the most programming in the name of children's or family ministries. This is why family ministry, as the U.S. Catholic Bishops described it in 1987, is, at its best, a perspective. As a perspective or a way of seeing things, family ministry is not simply another program for the church; nor is it a specialty for the religious professional. Even the best programs, like medicines, are good here and there, but they easily become the quick fix and if overprescribed can do more harm than good. Family ministry as a perspective, however, views virtually all dimensions of religious and community life and considers them in light of their impact and influence on families.

Just as businesses and developers have to do an analysis of the environmental impact of proposed projects, congregations would do well to reflect on the family impact of new projects or even established ones. Is worship yet another time to divvy families up? Or can it be time together for them? How about religious education? How does our schedule of committee meetings affect family life? Would having them at someone's home help or make matters worse? What are we doing to our rabbi's family? What impact will this job description, if carried out, have on the minister's children? What are some alternative ways to help families—ways that don't take over their time or dignity? Should we consider de-programming ourselves? Or maybe we need programs but in a different direction. What are we doing well? How are we already serving families constructively? Can we build on these strengths? These are the kinds of questions that a family perspective brings and to which a family program can be blind. They are important ones for parents themselves to consider, as it is often parents who are sitting on the decision-making committees and boards of congregations themselves. And such questions may indeed lead to new or transformed programs. Imagining family ministry as a perspective invites reflection before programming.

BRAIDING

In an essay documenting and reflecting on family ministry in a Boston-area synagogue, Brita Gill-Austern describes the importance of home and family life, working in conjunction with the congregation. "Traditionally," she explains, "Judaism has been passed on through the generations, not primarily by participation in the synagogue, but by faithful familial observance of Shabbat and other Jewish holidays and rituals." Gill-Austern goes on to point out that "Judaism is not learned first through cognitive acquisition of concepts or principles, but through the repetition and participation in ritual observance in family life."

I once spoke at a retreat for ministers and directors of religious education where I naively lobbed out similar ideas in relation to Christianity and the church: parents are educators; family life teaches, and so on. The group nodded politely but was fairly silent. After a break, the leader of the group finally spoke up, reflecting a panic that was settling in. He said, "This sounds good, but what would *we* do? I mean this is our job!"

Before that moment, I had never considered how paying attention to parents and home life for educational ministry might actually be a threat to professional ministry. The leader was just being honest. And being the bright, creative people they were, these congregational leaders soon were answering their own questions, saying such things as this: "Well, maybe we could help parents in this role. A lot of families would have no idea how to begin observing religious rituals outside of church. What about single people? Maybe they can be godparents if they want, or they could adopt their own 'families.' Maybe we could do more home-based studies or small groups. We could recruit some older parents to work with new parents. Or we could extend the (infant) baptism classes to really emphasize the role of family in the baptismal vows. And what if we got the parents involved more heavily in the youth group. . . . " And so it went. In all, they were reflecting the very attitude of the Beth El congregation that Gill-Austern describes. "The synagogue does not try to take over the role of the parents, but to support, undergird, and give them resources to do their job raising Jewish children. The synagogue's job is to empower and teach parents the tools to model a Jewish way of life for their children."

Although I might have been able to give these professionals at the retreat one or two ideas myself, I continually find that congregational leaders and practitioners, given half a chance to reflect, will come up with twenty good ideas for any one idea an outsider might have. They know their people, their congregation, their community, their households; they know what might work, what might not, what they are already doing well, and what they can build on. There is always plenty of work to do, but the work may shift its emphasis as a different perspective settles in. Families can benefit powerfully through the resources of the larger community, even while families themselves can strengthen congregations. Family ministry at Beth El operates with the conviction that "without Jewish children the braid of generations and of Judaism breaks." Beneath this is an even deeper conviction, in the words of Beth El's rabbi Kushner, "that we meet God in the faces of our parents and in the faces of our children." He says, "We meet God in the cycle of generations."

DEFINING A CONGREGATION

Like a good relationship of any sort, the relationship between homes and congregations has a power greater than the sum of the parts. So turn about is fair play. We can ask ourselves about the meaning of congregations, too. Skipping the task of trying to define them (congregations are deep, too) we can ask:

What makes a congregation a congregation? Name specific activities, attitudes, or events. _____

_____

Or another way into the matter is this:

Some of the most meaningful experiences in congregations have been

_____

_____

Again, remembering stories and revealing moments can be powerful glimpses into the meaning of congregational experiences for people.

Like the Apostle Paul, many people speak of the importance of the love and care they have experienced. Congregations have been rich sources of hope, courage, and grace for many, especially when they were going through hard times or facing cruel treatment or prejudice in the larger community. Lots of people name worship, prayer, or a sense of the Spirit at work as crucial to congregations. In turn, these evoke awe, praise, gratitude, and a sense of grace and salvation. Others name having a sense of meaning, being part of a larger community, or living in a place where they can give something back to the community or be part of a large service effort like Habitat for Humanity or fighting global hunger or poverty. Often people focus on the big celebrations or holidays. Others name the message or sermon or the chance to study scriptures with others and to learn from those who have studied a lot. Some have found their greatest friendships through congregations. Parents often say how important it is that they can trust their children to others there and for their children to develop meaningful relationships with other adults. Some have found, through congregations, the power to turn their lives around and overcome self-destructive ways. Music is huge for many. Food pops up a lot in stories of sharing in pot-luck dinners or feeding others. Some say it is a chance "to get out of myself and my everyday worries," whereas I have heard others say, "I feel more myself, more at home." As is the case with family experiences, some people have had extremely painful experiences in congregations, and they are hoping for something better. Most people resist narrowing the meaning of congregational life into one thing. Or if they do, it quickly spills into more. Worship spills into community, which spills into prayer, which spills into the message.

Overall, most people find it helpful and encouraging to share the meaning and power they experience through congregational life. When parents are racing around trying to get everyone out the door on time for service, when the teenager complains, or when you've given up your day off to go build a home for someone, reminders of the meaning of such commitments can help motivate and sustain us through the hassles. When the child asks, "Why do I have to go?" you may not think of all this on the spot. You may simply say, "Because it's something we do." But it helps to remind yourself now and then why and at a less stressful time be able to share the meaning.

One of the most powerful stories that I have heard, expressing such meaning, does not come from a class or group discussion; it comes from scripture. It is a description of the early Christian community in Jerusalem:

They devoted themselves to the apostles' teaching and fellowship, to the breaking of bread and the prayers. Awe came upon everyone, because many wonders and signs were being done by the apostles. All who believed were together and had all things in common; they would sell their possessions and goods and distribute the proceeds to all, as any had need. Day by day, as they spent much time together in the temple, they broke bread at home and ate their food with glad and generous hearts, praising God and having the goodwill of all the people. And day by day the Lord added to their number those who were being saved [Acts 2:43–47].

Awe, wonder, sharing goods and possessions, caring for needs—these are marks of spiritual community. Teaching and learning, breaking bread, spending time together—this is spiritual territory. Praise, fellowship, prayer, glad and generous hearts—the wonderful reality is, these things can happen in congregations and homes alike; they happen all the time. Notice how the spiritual lines between homes and congregations soften as deep sources of meaning are recognized in each realm and in the relationship between them.

FINDING THE MEANING OF HOME

So what's in a home? A lot. In the book *The Meaning of Things,* the authors reflect on a large number of interviews with families regarding what makes home a home. They conclude from their research that "the home is not only a material shelter but also a shelter for those things that make life meaningful." Our homes shelter meaning.

Biblically, in the story of faith, we saw home explode with meaning. Home could include the doorposts of a house as well as the promised homeland. Home could include households of worship or even creation. Congregations can be like home, and they may assemble in literal houses. We saw this with families as well. Families are rooted in marriages, births, and genealogies. But they also emerge through attachment, community, and adoption just as easily. Over and over again, faith presses our hearts and minds in two directions fundamental to life. One is near, the other far. Faith treasures the reality right before our eyes: our children, family time, and the doorposts to our material lives. Faith also takes our attention to the wider contexts of living and meaning: extended family, neighborhoods, congregations, nations, and creation, for example. Meaning itself seems to have this double-sided nature: concrete and symbolic, specific and general, visible and invisible, particular and universal, part and whole. Faith sees meaning through this double vision.

In terms of the relationship between homes and congregations, this double vision can guide the way for appreciating how each realm enhances the other. Congregations and their programming life can be careful to value the integrity of family life and support it, as the Beth El congregation works to do, or families can discover wider contexts of meaning if they see themselves in a larger world of concern. Two situations from my own congregation illustrate what I mean.

My tradition practices confirmation—a rite celebrating the Holy Spirit's confirmation of one's baptism. In the Protestant tradition, confirmation is a time of intense religious education. Typically, it happens in adolescence and is prepared for through homework and classes; in my denomination's curriculum, this includes a daily scripture study. The year our son David was to be confirmed, a seminary student taught the course. She wanted to get parents more involved in the whole affair, so she gently but persuasively encouraged parents to do the Bible study *with* their children. Some parents had to work out arrangements with their divorced spouses; some were grandparents or godparents; some were faithful about it and others were not. For ourselves, we were fairly regular with David, some evenings having to cover the two or three nights we had missed earlier. Other nights, the study or conversation or prayer felt uninspired. Cora joined us sometimes, sometimes not. At first the task was a little burdensome, but over time, devoting some time to reading scripture, talking about it, and praying became a treasured time for us. Frankly, it made it easier to talk about God at other times. (Talking about God, many parents find, can be extremely difficult.) And when confirmation day came, I believe the experience was even more meaningful than it would have been otherwise—for all of us.

This confirmation class was a simple situation of re-imagining how a program of the congregation could be carried out in a way that valued the integrity and power of family relationships. The class involved no new programs, no new materials, no extra money. Our church simply asked us to spend a little more time together.

Another situation involves a family spending time together but in service to a larger concern of the congregation. Our congregation has been part of a larger community effort to help find homes and work for refugees coming from the Sudan. These were boys orphaned by the war and left with no families, homes, or anything else; they had simply been surviving the best they could and were now young men. As I watched Cora make a beautiful sign to welcome the young men our congregation was helping to re-settle, I thought about how important that was to her own religious education. She was, in a sense, learning that faith is concerned about people all over the world. But I was struck even more poignantly one Sunday after church, when several of us were moving some furniture into an apartment that was to house some of the young men. One couple had their young children with them, carrying some of the smaller items: silverware, a pan, a pocket dictionary. As they were walking up the third flight of stairs, their four-year-old girl asked, "Why are we bringing all this stuff?"

The mother answered, "Because they don't have anything."

"Nothing?"

Mom replied, "Nothing."

The girl's eyes got very wide. She realized for the first time that some people have not a thing.

Educators call these teachable moments. They are moments in everyday life that present themselves and are ripe for learning. But in this case we can notice how the everyday life of this family, by being woven into a congregation and its concerns, took a family and its children into a larger world of meaning. This little girl got an early lesson in "nothingness," as well as a caring community's response. Homes shelter materials; homes shelter refugees; homes shelter meaning.

LOOKING AHEAD

The next two chapters continue our exploration of the implications of the double vision of faith and the ways in which families with children can become more intentional about cultivating the life of faith. I believe there are intentional, concrete activities that help children see life in deeper ways. And I believe there are ways of seeing that help children know a securing power that sets everyday living free.

Chapter 8

THE JOY OF PRACTICE

My (now teenage) son and I embarked on an adventure a few years ago that reminds me again what can happen through learning. Together we have been learning to play the conga drums. As we began, we were both starting from scratch in relation to percussion, and I had not had a music lesson since I was eight years old. Linda, our talented and patient teacher, has been amazingly helpful and encouraging. Typically, she introduces a rhythm to us by playing it. The music itself inspires us, stirring the hope in us that we will be able to play likewise. Then she breaks the rhythm down into its parts—right hand, left hand, high drum, low, slap, bass tone, touch—and so it goes. Our homework is to practice putting these parts together so we can play the full rhythm for her the next week. Not only does Linda know how to teach by showing us the relationship between part and whole, she does something else that is crucial to good learning. She makes it fun. The experience reminds me again of the sheer joy of learning.

Good learning reinforces itself. Fun, joy, meaning—all create a constructive loop that motivates us to devote the time and energy it takes to practice or work on learning. In the case of our drumming, having some fun with it, together, was a key reason we wanted to play in the first place. But the joy of learning runs deeper than fun. There is something about learning itself—learning something where there was nothing, learning to perform, attaining a skill, developing a gift —that is inherently meaningful. It could be learning to drum or learning to whistle; it could be learning to cook or learning the history of rose gardening; it could be learning to read or learning to ride a bicycle. All such learning is gratifying. The more complex and demanding, the greater the gratification, as long as there are successes along the way. My hunch is that the joy of learning has to do with tapping our deepest natures, with tapping our freedom, creativity, and love for life. As we learn, our wonderful strangeness, our openness to possibilities finds a home where it can thrive.

THE WORLD OF PRACTICE

Without joy or meaning, sustaining the discipline and practice that learning requires is all but impossible. The tasks of learning become overwhelming burdens. However, when the joy of learning happens, even the "burdens" can be meaningful. Even practice. A friend of mine is a seasoned opera singer, and he still spends many hours a week training his voice and practicing his art, even when he is not performing publicly. I asked him how he stays motivated, and he responded, "When I practice I get to sing, and I love to sing." I can imagine no greater sense of meaning, joy, or gratification in learning than when the practice itself is joy. When practice and learning are always for the sake of something else—for performing, for mastery, for getting a good grade, for getting a job—the sheer enjoyment of the activity can get lost in such functional goals.

Something else happens in practice that is part of this gratifying loop that motivates and sustains learning: subtleties emerge. As subtleties emerge, as complexities and nuances are appreciated, the world gets richer and practice takes on depth. In fact, practice itself opens new realms. In terms of drumming, practice is not only a matter of putting parts together but discovering new possibilities. Maybe I get a slight popping sound when my hand is cupped a bit more. Maybe a tiny delay in timing or omission of a beat turns the whole rhythm in a new direction. Perhaps starting with my left hand makes the third beat stand out a little more. The world of the drum turns out to be much more complex and fascinating than either David or I ever realized. But these discoveries, these complexities and possibilities keep the learning fresh and sustain the time and effort it takes to sit down and play. The discoveries and subtleties of learning are ingredients for the joy of learning.

While the world becomes more subtle through learning, learning also makes the world bigger. As David and I got better at learning particular rhythms, Linda began playing recordings for us. She taught us how to listen for particular rhythms in relation to specific songs and then connect them to more general styles of music. Eventually, we were able to work on the beat and play along with the recordings. To help with this process, she has passed along tapes and CDs from her own collection and has even taken us to hear local bands play. Linda is Puerto Rican by heritage and emphasizes all kinds of Latin beats and music. (It is not surprising to find David falling asleep at night listening to this music.) The point is that, even as our appreciation for the subtleties of rhythms deepens, our cultural-musical world grows beyond a four-four rock backbeat.

In addition, learning the drums affects how we see; better, it affects how we hear and feel the world around us. In the natural world, as well as in the cultural world, there is rhythm all over the place. In breathing air or gulping a glass of water, there is rhythm; in a bird's song or a train's rumble there is rhythm. Rhythm is everywhere. It was always there, but now we are much more likely to notice. Driving down the road, I sometimes catch my son working out the rhythm for the song on the radio. As he slaps his knees, he might say, "Sounds almost like a samba beat, but just a little different here." Or he might say, "That's the same beat we learned last week." I have been affected, too. Often now, out on a long walk or run, I hear rhythms in my mind playing off the cadence of my stride. Sometimes I catch myself practicing on my chest, working out a new challenge or experimenting in relation to my steps.

This may be more than you want to know about the world of drumming, but there are clues about any kind of learning in the example of learning to play the congas. There are also clues about the relationship between practice, learning, and meaning. In general, practice sustains learning. This is obvious to most people. But less obvious is the way in which practice actually generates learning and, along with it, meaning.

SPIRITUAL PRACTICE

This book has devoted a lot of attention to issues of why: why faith matters, why families and homes resist definition, why raising children in faith is important, why sin happens, and why perspectives on life and ministries can make a difference. All of these issues affect motivation for the religious life. Without addressing the deeper questions of meaning and faith, spiritual practices easily degenerate into burdens and busyness in a world already overloaded with things to do. Practice requires time, discipline, and energy. Practice is demanding, and this is as true for the spiritual life as it is for learning to play music. So if practice is disconnected from questions of meaning, practice will drain our time and energy. Or if practice is so oriented to functional goals that we no longer say, "I get to sing," then it will eventually go flat.

In the spiritual life, generally, practice is understood in a couple of ways. On the one hand, if you are a "practicing" Christian or Jew, you are the opposite of a "lapsed" Christian or "unobservant" Jew. Practicing means doing things out of faith; maybe you pray, worship, or serve others. On the other hand, the term *practice* also refers to specific activities; praying, worshiping, or serving are each considered to be spiritual practices. In this sense, we focus time and energy to engage in some particular activity. In the larger sense of practice, we focus time and energy to engage our lives in an overall way. In both senses of the word, practice gives texture to the life of faith.

Both senses of practice are helpful to remember as we raise our children. Practice involves specific activities; practice is a general orientation to life. When practices are only specific activities like prayer or worship, it is easier to locate them in one place, such as in a congregation. But when linked to a whole lifestyle, it is easier to imagine and engage in practices anywhere and everywhere. Prayer can happen at home; caring can happen for those in another country.

The reason for noticing these ways of understanding practice is that one of the most powerful ways in which parents can be spiritual teachers is through practice. In this case, teaching is not so much oriented to drawing out three points of a Bible lesson or helping a child memorize a catechism, though it can include these. Again, parents have to shake off images of teaching shaped by classroom education. A powerful form of teaching is simply leading the way for engaging in rituals, disciplines, and practices that are explicitly religious. When these happen at home, children learn that home is spiritual territory. Not only do they communicate that a family can be a community of faith, practices connect the family community to the congregational community. Children learn that prayer, for example, is not just something that happens at worship, but it happens at the dinner table. Children can learn that talk of God is not just something that happens in religion classes or Sunday schools but on a front porch or in a car. Religious practices are bigger than either a congregation or a home, so they can unite both realms.

There is no doubt that the greatest challenge to practicing faith at home has to do with the multiple demands and complexity of modern (or postmodern) family life. We are a scattered lot, and nearly everything in contemporary society wants to drive us apart more. And as I noted in the previous chapter, even religion can add to this fragmenting mania, especially as it divides families and communities up by developmental stages or categories of special concern. But religion does not have to be divisive. In fact, the scattering of community life in the contemporary world only highlights the importance of families and communities finding ways to do things together. Religious practice at home, in congregations, in the community can have binding power, and we desperately need it. We need the kinds of practice that focus life together and resist the hurried manipulations spawned by a consumption-obsessed economy and technological culture. We can bless our children by showing them rhythms of life not driven by shopping, electronics, hurrying, fleeting images, working longer hours, fast meals, quick fixes, and speed in general. Although this hyper-world is not likely to change any time soon, the rhythms of the life of faith may slow us down long enough for creative possibilities to emerge.

Parents have to decide for themselves how and what they want to do in the way of faith practices in the home. I will suggest some possibilities because, historically, some activities continually emerge in the world of faith—perennial activities that can happen in congregations and homes alike. Over and again, practices involving prayer, the reading of sacred texts, service, talk of God, meals, and celebration emerge in faith communities in one way or another. Very often these activities occur in conjunction with one another; each can be carried out in a thousand different ways, according to various traditions. And there are many, many more kinds of rituals and expressions of the spiritual life that are also very important (for example, rituals of confession and atonement or anointing and healing). I offer some ideas about the role of particular traditions and rituals in home life in the next chapter. For now, I want to highlight some more general activities that can be carried out in the midst of family life.

PRAYER

When a child sees a father bow his head in prayer or a mother raise her hands in praise, the child is learning to see that there is an authority even greater than the parent. As one child put it, God is "her parents' parent." The child is learning a lot about humility; the child is learning a lot about a source of security even greater than the parent.

Prayer itself covers a wide range of concerns and, as it does, integrates a wide range of human life, from joys to concerns, in relation to the Holy. Prayers of praise and prayers of thanksgiving teach gratitude. Prayers of concern teach about care and sources of strength in hard times. Prayers in hushed tones or silence teach reverence and respect; exuberant prayer teaches passion and joy. As children themselves pray, not only are they practicing these things but they can reveal what may be going on in their souls. A child may be afraid to start school, need protection from a bully, be so thankful for Grandma, or hope people who are hungry can find some bread today. Hearing the prayers of our children teaches us about them, helps us pay attention, helps us know how they are doing.

A few years ago, when Jane's father was battling leukemia, we heard a great many prayers from our children: " . . . and God be with Grandpa, help him get better." Sometimes the prayer would extend, " . . . and be with everyone who is sick or dying." Prayer created a place where they could share their worries with God and with us. Sometimes we would talk about Grandpa; sometimes we could not and had to let tears speak for us. But this is what prayer so often does. It creates a place for our fears and joys, a place to share vulnerabilities and sources of comfort. I know some parents worry, "What if our children pray for something, like healing, and it doesn't happen. What will that say about God?" My only response to parents regarding this concern is that prayer also gives us a place to live with the ambiguities of life such as addressing a God we miss or hoping that those who are dying will heal. Jane's father, Andy, after some valiant fighting, lost the battle after a year or so. The prayers of David and Cora shifted a bit: " . . . and God, be with Grandma and with Mom." It seems to me that a good practice—in this case, the practice of prayer—is big enough to handle the ambiguities, the fears, and the concerns of life, and even death itself. And by engaging in such practices, we can handle them better, too. In fact, a few months later, after Andy's death, Cora offered a prayer at dinner. "Dear God," she prayed, "tell Grandpa we miss him, but tell him we're doing okay."

Prayer, like other religious activities, can be done alone. And this is helpful for children to know and to learn. But I am suggesting that families pray together, too. Many parents do have a prayer or devotional life, but it is completely hidden from their children. I am suggesting opening that life up a bit and sharing it. Sharing experiences together is a large part of their binding power. There are no guarantees that "families that pray together stay together," because some families that pray together still fall apart. But I do think prayer is an integrating force holding communities together. It connects the parts to a larger whole. And so it is with the other practices as well. Shared meals and celebrations, as well as reading and talking together, help families and congregations stay together.

Because prayer can touch the deepest vulnerabilities in our lives, because prayer can be such an intimate experience, prayer can also be very intimidating. On the one hand, it can be so personal; on the other, we are addressing the Holy Creator of the universe, whose name we are forbidden to utter. This is powerful business. So it is no wonder that many parents, like many people in general, are afraid or overwhelmed to share in prayer with others, even family members. I hear from parents, "I'm not sure what to say anyway. Then with my children listening, I'm even more scared." I believe this is another area where the resources of one's congregation and tradition can be very helpful. Every religious tradition practices prayer in its own way. Some emphasize speaking from the heart; others emphasize formal, historical, or memorized prayers. I suggest taking your cues from your congregation's tradition and resources. Almost any congregation can put you in touch with resources for prayer. Many have devotional books that are designed for individual use but can easily be used in family settings. Libraries, bookstores, religious magazines, and even the Internet are loaded with resources. One of the most empowering forms of family ministry a congregation can offer is to make resources available for use outside the congregational walls. If nothing else, most congregations use some sort of worship bulletin or worship book full of prayers. Pay attention to these, and you should find plenty of help. Families could easily use, say, a prayer of thanksgiving printed in a worship bulletin as a mealtime blessing all week. Another great resource is the Bible itself, particularly the Book of Psalms, which is a book full of prayers. The Psalms have been one of the most meaningful guides to prayer in our household. Not only do they provide something to say, they put us in touch with the wisdom and history of people thousands of years ago.

For those who are motivated but not comfortable with praying aloud, using printed words can be a great way to practice prayer. It lets us do something on the one hand; on the other, it is a way of gaining facility with prayer, a way of getting accustomed to saying words of prayer in front of others, a way of learning. And so it is with children. If they hear us pray, if they learn to say prayers themselves, they will be much more comfortable with prayer and perhaps discover subtleties and meaning through it.

SACRED TEXTS

Parents reach a magic point in their family lives when their children learn to read for themselves. Although Jane and I thoroughly enjoyed Dr. Seuss and *Goodnight Moon,* as well as all kinds of other stories and poems, after the first two or three thousand times through, enough was enough. When the children could read to themselves at night, it was a source of pride for them and a wonderful relief for us. Having said this, it caught me off-guard one night, two or three years after we had quit reading to our children, when David asked me to read, out loud, a poem from a book he had. I did.

He asked, "How 'bout another one?"

"Okay." I read another. This time Cora slipped in and started listening.

She said, "Do another one." So I read a few more; then I suggested they each read one and then get to bed.

The next night, they asked to repeat the reading. And each night after, they kept asking. I was getting worried; I thought I was done with this. So before long I was talking Jane into relieving me of this duty, which had strangely returned from the past. But after a couple nights of relief, I found myself slipping in and listening, too. Finally, we gave into this impulse and started by all sitting down together and reading books or stories or poems out loud together. Except for some breaks here and there, we've been reading out loud ever since.

Because Jane and I were so tired of reading the same preschool stories over and over again, we had forgotten the magic of reading out loud and the special time with the children reading had initially been. The hardest part for us now is choosing the next book. Sometimes we find ourselves not able to make the time to read together; someone is out of town, we have late meetings, or homework is not finished. But the truth is, we seem to find it harder to make some time to read when the book itself is not particularly good. The better the book, the more likely we are to decide not to watch a television show instead, or make a phone call, or get papers graded, or check e-mail. Meaningful time, like good learning, is self-reinforcing and even has a way of creating time.

The first part of this book emphasized the importance of scriptures, of faith's story and the ways in which it roots us in faith. The scriptures, in fact, are so pivotal in a living faith that reading them can begin to feel like a duty. And maybe it is. But doing things out of duty alone has a way of killing the joy. So I share with you the experience of reading aloud with our children to accentuate another dimension of reading sacred texts: the sheer power of words and stories shared aloud. Some families make daily scripture reading a part of their lives. It could be as simple as a passage from a devotional book, accompanied with a prayer. It could be reading from a children's Bible at bedtime. Some make it a weekly habit, accompanied by a Friday evening or Sunday meal, for example. A friend of mine tells of the sense of reverence created when his father would go get the Bible from the shelf, open it, and begin reading. "There was just something about it, almost visceral, it felt real." This friend, a preacher, has devoted his life to exploring and sharing that reality.

Because the Bible is such a big book, the challenge is figuring out where to begin or how to find some kind of approach through it. Again, congregations, libraries, and bookstores usually have resource materials to help. Many people find it helpful to simply repeat the scripture readings covered in worship or class or Bible study. Unlike most preschool reading, going back over a passage of scripture that has been preached or taught usually reveals subtleties missed the first time. Parents can also pick the brains of the professionals, congregational leaders, or friends they respect. A parenting group, if there is one in the congregation, can play a helpful role. I know one group that, instead of focusing on how to get their children to behave or get to bed or all the other daily concerns of parents, did a Bible study. The study was intended to prepare the parents to read the passages with their own children. Inevitably, issues of discipline or the frustrations of parenting arose, but they were placed in a larger perspective. In this case, reading sacred texts had binding power in family life, as parents read with their children, but also binding power with others in the congregation.

MEALS

Food has always been an important vehicle for sacred learning. The bitter herbs of a Passover seder teach about the bitterness of slavery in Egypt. The broken bread of communion teaches the crucifixion. Kosher laws, potluck dinners, meals for the grieving or ill, *Shabbat,* and Sunday dinner—these meals teach so much, including what it means to be part of this community, part of this family. Anthropologists pay particular attention to what happens around food in a society because so often the patterns and values of the society come to a head around the meal. The world-famous twentieth-century psychologist Erik Erikson would always try to have a meal with a family before treating a child. He wanted to see what was going on in the society of that child's family, and the meal was a good way to find out.

In fact, it was through meals that early Christianity and early Judaism in the first century distinguished themselves from the surrounding Greco-Roman culture. At the festival meals and banquets of the Greco-Romans, it was expected that slaves, women, and children would not even attend unless it was to serve the property-owning men. In other words, the practices around the meal reflected the hierarchy of society; property-owning men were considered to be more deserving of love, respect, honor, and food itself. But then certain Jewish movements, including Christianity, challenged such ranking systems and, in turn, meals were eaten in a different way. These movements would try to accommodate large numbers of people rather than an honored few; they would insist on equality in relationships, and the numbers would include women and children. Jesus, for example, tells people not to choose places of honor at a banquet. In fact, he says, "When you give a banquet, invite the poor, the crippled, the lame, and the blind" (Luke 14). Such teaching would turn the ranking system on its head. A more contemporary example would be the lunch counters and dining halls of the 1960s. Freedom Riders risked their lives to transform America's laws about eating, about who could break bread together. For a white person and a black person to sit together at the same table and share a meal was not just something nice to do; it was a revolution. So meals are more than food. They teach and sustain a community's values.

For many households, the dinner table is a place that gathers the family and more. It may gather other sacred practices as well: a prayer, a scripture reading, or holiday celebration, for example. A friend told me of a ritual her own busy family has for supper. They light a candle, both for aesthetics and as "a reminder of God's light." After receiving a Bible from her congregation in third grade, her daughter has been reading from the Psalms, just a few verses. They take turns praying, but the other child likes to write and, with the encouragement of a Sunday School teacher, has written some prayers the family uses before the meal. As my friend told me about this, I thought it all sounded a bit too idyllic, so I had several questions:

"Does she understand those psalms?"

"Not always, but she will."

"I see."

"On the other hand, I don't always either; sometimes we talk about it; sometimes it's probably just a thoughtless ritual."

"What are the prayers like?"

"Some make me cringe; some are beautiful—a little like the psalms when I think about it."

"You all sound too good; don't you all fight or anything?"

"Who said we didn't? Who said we were good? We fuss all the time. Hell, the other night the kids got in a big argument over who would light the candle! Sometimes we argue; sometimes we tell jokes. We laugh, cry, bicker, act like babies, act like adults. Sometimes it's great; sometimes it's kinda boring. The point is—I'm not sure what the point is. We're just together. It's us. I don't think about it in terms of good and bad."

This mother may not think of the mealtime in terms of good and bad. But of particular interest to parents of older children and youth are studies pointing to the constructive role that family meals play in the lives of teenagers. Research out of The National Center on Addiction and Substance Abuse at Columbia University suggests that the odds of teenagers doing drugs go down as they eat with their parents.

The odds that 12- to 17-year-olds will smoke, drink or use marijuana rise as the number of meals they have with their parents declines. Only six percent of kids who eat dinner with their parents six or more times a week smoke compared with 24 percent of those who eat dinner with their parents twice a week or less; for marijuana use, it's 12 percent compared with 35 percent.

The research also gives insight into the current debate about whether parents or peers are more formative for children. "Kids who do not smoke pot credit their parents with their decision; kids who smoke pot credit their peers." Significantly, the other most helpful factor for preventing drug use is religion, specifically, attending religious services. Now there is nothing magical or mechanical about eating meals or attending services that automatically wards off these behaviors. It is more the case that eating together and participating in religious practices are part of a larger fabric of living. "Parents who eat meals with their kids know where they are after school and on weekends and are involved in their children's school activities and academics."

So my suggestion is to eat together. Give the children chores in the meal's preparation and cleanup. Turn off televisions and telephones, say a prayer, enjoy the food, bicker, fuss, joke, and cherish the company. Meals are sacred.

SERVICE

Whether it is preparing a home for homeless refugees or paying a visit to a homebound neighbor, acts of service teach children to care for others. Care is practiced within the home, just as it is within a congregation. But if it stays only in the home or congregation, children miss the greatest mission of faith itself, that is, to serve a hurting world. Each act of care and compassion teaches a child more than we can say. Some congregations facilitate the possibilities for service by organizing mission trips or having ongoing tasks such as taking flowers or meals to the elderly, volunteering at a shelter, or advocating for vulnerable people. Most congregations provide ample opportunities. My primary suggestion for parents and congregational leaders is to look for situations where it could be appropriate to include children. Could the mission trip be an intergenerational one? A child may be too young to work at the Habitat for Humanity building site, but could he or she help make sandwiches to feed the workers?

The national champion of vulnerable children, Marian Wright Edelman, tells of growing up in a household that valued service to others and how these values she learned so early shape her work with the Children's Defense Fund. In her home, "children were taught," she says, "not by sermonizing, but by personal example—that nothing was too lowly to do." She goes on to tell about a debate her parents had when she was eight or nine: Was young Marian too young to go with her older brother Harry to clean the bed and bedsores of a sick, poor woman? She remembers, "I went and learned just how much the smallest helping hands and kindness can mean to a person in need."

I am not suggesting that the main reason to engage in acts of service is to teach our children something. The main reason is to bring care and compassion to where it is needed. The same is true with other sacred practices. We engage in them for their own sake. Nonetheless, there are some indirect fruits of these practices. They are times together, they generate meaning, they forge deep bonds, they root our lives in deep soil, they resist the powers that hurry and fragment human relationships. And yes, these practices teach. We and our children can learn through them. So in terms of the practice of serving and caring, children not only receive care from their parents and communities, they can learn to give it and to bring care into another generation.

Personally, I believe acts of service teach the deepest lessons in the mystery of others and, consequently, are one of the greatest weapons against evil. The worst atrocities humanity commits against itself occur by dehumanizing others, that is, by reducing the fullness (mystery) of others to problems. Racism, genocide, torture, and violence in general all illustrate and embody the point. But compassion works in precisely the opposite direction. People are not problems, not reducible, not to be treated like dirt. Acts of service teach our children that every human being is made in the image of God. Acts of care teach the holiness of others.

TALK OF GOD

Talking of God is not always easy; in fact, I don't think it should be. We can cheapen respect for God through cursing, for example, but we can also do so through facile explanations and easy theological answers: "God didn't want me to have that parking spot" or "Your suffering is a gift from the Lord." Nonetheless, talking of God is important. If God is only mentioned in congregational life, it is difficult for children to see the sacred possibilities of everyday living.

Talking of God is more than simply using words for the Holy One or more than praying to God. Talking of God is akin to talking about what we believe, what our convictions are—things that really matter and fire passionate concern. It is also akin to talking about big issues—matters of life and death, suffering and joy, or love and care. For children to be in an atmosphere where God can be revered as well as discussed teaches children how to deal with all kinds of important matters with respect and confidence. Sex, conflict, politics, and ethical dilemmas, for example, can all be difficult to discuss.

As with praying, many parents are intimidated by God talk because they are not sure what to say. "Maybe I'll say the wrong thing." "I don't know why bad things happen to good people." "I'm not sure what to think of miracles." Because talking of God is so closely related to big life-and-death issues that resist easy answers, a simple question from a child can raise some of our own deepest questions and theological struggles. Sometimes it is easier to say, "Ask your rabbi" or "Ask the minister." And there may be times when asking would be a wonderful thing to do, perhaps together. But if referring to others is the main strategy for God questions and God talk, children learn that home is not a place for discussing deep issues or difficult matters. In addition, if you do not already know this, clergy struggle with these big questions, too, and they may be no better prepared to talk to a child about them than anyone else.

One of the best pieces of advice that anyone gave me, as a parent, about such matters was this: don't be so sure your child always needs an answer. So instead of having an elaborate discussion about transcendence or referring your child to the clergy, perhaps it is enough to say, "I'm not sure why we can't see God. What do you think?" Many times this is all the child wants—a chance to wonder openly about things or express an idea. The simple response, "I'm not sure. What do you think?" can open the door to a meaningful conversation, and a child learns that home is a good place to reflect on such matters, that the child's questions and thoughts are taken seriously, and that there are big questions in life that don't always go away. Yes, parents need to be very clear with children about some things: "You do not cross that road by yourself," "You will wear your helmet when you ride your bicycle," "You and the car will be home by five o'clock." Clarity in these matters secures safety. And there are also matters of conviction to be clear about: "We do not use that word in this house," "I believe with all my heart that God loves you," "It is wrong to judge people by skin color." But there are other matters in life that are not so clear, so we can model how to live with difficult or even unanswerable questions.

On top of all of this, the truth is that sometimes we will give bad answers. Sometimes we will fail at negotiating a good conversation. Sometimes we will not listen carefully enough or we will be too tired to realize that a perfect moment to talk about God or something important just flew by. Parents need to be gracious to themselves as well as others. And children can learn by such grace. Without a context of grace, any and all of these practices can feed an abiding sense of failure, which in turn fuels anxious living, which is the wrong spirit. And even in a good spirit, there are no guarantees. It is easy to convince ourselves that, "If I pray daily with my child, she will be a better person" or "If we read the Bible together, my son will be more faithful."

The Power of God at Home

However, religious learning and the religious life, generally, are simply not mechanical enterprises with neat cause-and-effect relationships. Nonetheless, even if our kids rebel against our values and beliefs, I would rather give them something meaningful to rebel against than a haunting void.

Then again, do not underestimate the power that any religious practice, including talk of God, may hold for a child. Author and musician James McBride tells how he asked his mother, walking home from church one day, whether God was black or white. McBride's mother was a Jewish immigrant from Europe; his father was an African American Baptist preacher. The question held high identity stakes for the child. His mother answered that God is not black or white but a spirit. But McBride pressed, "Does he like black or white people better?"

"He loves all people. He's a spirit."

"What's a spirit?"

"A spirit's a spirit."

"What color is God's spirit?"

"It doesn't have a color," she said. "God is the color of water. Water doesn't have a color."

For the young McBride, thinking of God as the color of water carried deep power and meaning for him through his young life and struggle for identity. Such "teachable moments" are spontaneous times when no one would have predicted that a deep lesson could be learned. But even though these are unplanned, it does seem to be true that teachable moments are more likely to emerge in homes where religious practices have been integrated into family life. If the subject of God is always avoided, it will be difficult for a child to ask God questions, especially the older they get. Praying, having thoughtful discussions, or reading scriptures, for example, can create an atmosphere where religious teachable moments are more likely to happen. And as McBride's conversation with his mother illustrates, talk of God can pave the way for talking about other kinds of deeply personal, highly charged matters.

CELEBRATION

Remember the joy of learning? Celebration is to the religious life as joy is to learning. Holidays and holy days, feasts and festivals, all help to sustain the life of faith. They order and shape the flow of the religious year. Christmas and Easter or Passover and Yom Kippur, for example, are times when religious communities remember and celebrate the presence of God, the Holy One who sustains life itself. These special times are not purely about joy and celebration, however. They also commemorate times of pain and suffering. For example, Easter recalls the crucifixion; Passover recalls the oppression of slavery. But the struggles of life are placed in an even wider context of the goodness of life—resurrection, freedom, redemption, and love.

Many homes that have no other visible religious practices in their lives celebrate the major holidays. These can be an important building block for other religious practices. Maybe a family decides to have a prayer or devotional reading every night in preparation for Christmas. Maybe a sabbath ritual is built into a weekend meal. Perhaps a meal and good company are taken to a lonely home-bound neighbor on a holiday. Religious practices have a way of working well together, each nourishing another.

Celebration, like joy, is tricky in this culture, however. First of all, most of the major holidays are pulled into the circle of a consume-and-spend economy. This can kill the joy and draw the meaning right out of a celebration. Although shopping for gifts or cards can be fun, it can easily become a duty overloaded with high expectations, competition, and greed. Parents are the main barrier between their children and such a culture. Keeping holidays rooted in their religious significance is a major way of helping children know a source of joy more enduring than the latest fad in toys or computer games. But another tricky matter has to do with joy and celebration themselves. We don't always feel joyous; we don't always feel like celebrating. Maybe this is the first Christmas since Mom died; maybe I just lost my job; maybe I find the intensity of the holiday overwhelming and depressing; maybe I am battling depression in a world that wants me to be happy and cheery. These are difficult issues and can plague children as well as adults. This is where, again, I think the spiritual nature of holidays is better than the pop cultural versions. For people going through a challenging time, the struggles and suffering expressed in the holiday may become particularly meaningful. Stories of Jesus on the cross before Easter, of the wandering in the wilderness, of the bitterness of oppression, of the desire for atonement, or of the slaughter of the innocents at Christmas—all are powerful stories to tell. Or something as simple as reading scripture or having a prayer or serving somebody in need during a holiday can give the child or adult something deeper to connect with, a place that can meet the sadness. It is helpful for families to be sensitive to these tricky dimensions of celebrations so they can tailor holidays in ways to suit their own situations.

With these qualifications in mind, however, sometimes families need to cut loose and have a party, get away, take a trip, prepare a feast, dance, sing, or raise a toast to life. Vacations, trips, weddings, reunions, special meals, birthdays, the end of school year, anniversaries, graduations, games, a bike ride, or a picnic—any or all of these are ways of sustaining joy in family life and teaching children that life is very good. Here, often, adults have more to learn from children than the other way around. Children know how to play; adults, for all kinds of good and serious reasons, can easily forget. But play and joy are joined at the hip.

Many families create their own playful rituals, not only for holiday celebrations or anniversaries but throughout the week or school year. The ritual might be as simple as playing catch after work or school or having a game night once a week. Other families have special meals on certain nights: homemade pizzas or breakfast at suppertime. Some parents like to create individual times with each child; every Wednesday they might play tennis in the park; every Saturday they go for a hike. Some families have a special place they visit every year—a special camping spot, a beach, a home town. These rituals and traditions, rooted in the playful side of life, are often some of the most meaningful times in a family's life. Enjoy.

BUILDING ON STRENGTHS

A major principle in education is one helpful to family life and religious practice. The principle is this: *build on strengths.* In education, building on strengths means if a student is good with language, the teacher tailors assignments around the use of language for that student. When studying history, for example, ask the student to write a report, tell what happened to the class, or perhaps write up the historical event as if it were a newspaper article. If students are particularly expressive, active, or dramatic, have them act the historical event out. Ask musically inclined students to write a song about it. The idea is not that students uninterested in history should not learn history but that students learn better by approaching subject material through their gifts and interests. They are more likely to find the learning meaningful and, in turn, students are motivated to keep learning.

The implication for families and religious practice is that you can build on the strengths your family already has. If you manage to eat meals fairly regularly, perhaps mealtime would be a good time to read a psalm or engage in prayer. If you know how to do holidays and celebrations well, maybe you can share some of that playfulness with friends or colleagues or others who could use some joy in their lives. If you read to your child at bedtime, perhaps that would be a good time to read a Bible story, too, or to say a prayer after you read. If you already pray with your children at bedtime, maybe that would be a good time to have some simple conversations about God. If you are highly creative people and enjoy creating new rituals, do so in the name of faith. If you do not feel so original, talk to other parents or ask people you respect what their families did growing up. Like anything, religious practice in home life is easier if a child grows up with it from the start. But children, even teenagers, may be more open to something new than you imagine, especially if they can have a say in it. You may have to experiment. But what if you try a devotional time and it just falls flat? Instead of giving up, it could be a time to rethink how your family does it. Maybe it starts with some drumming, or a walk, or a really good book and ends with a favorite prayer or blessing.

There is nothing set in stone about the practices identified in this chapter. There are certainly more, and there are ways in which the list itself is artificial. If you have a practice of inviting new congregation members to your home for a holiday meal, and at the meal you say a prayer, what practice would this be? Sharing meals? Celebrating? Prayer? Service? Perhaps you would call it something else altogether: practicing hospitality? The important thing is for children to know that faith is meaningful to you as a parent and to you as a family. And because it is so important, you want to find ways to live it out and discover ways for it to become meaningful to them as well. You can build on the strength of your family relationships to express and live into the spiritual life, even as the spiritual life strengthens family relationships.

I think of these visible religious practices, done intentionally and regularly, as analogous to a sanctuary. Recall Abraham Heschel's statement: "Even those who believe that God is everywhere set aside a place for a sanctuary." He goes on, "For the sacred to be sensed at all moments everywhere, it must also at this moment be somewhere." Religious practices are the "somewheres" in home life that help us sense the sacred everywhere.

Chapter 9

SACRED CONNECTIONS

"I want to be the kind of writer," said poet and professor Ethelbert Miller in an interview, "the kind of person whose life becomes a poem." It was his answer to a question about why he spends so much time and energy devoted to community service and teaching in prisons. For Miller, poetry is a form of spirituality that is devoted to the work of love. He sees a connection between crafting words in beautiful and powerful ways and crafting life in beautiful and powerful ways. Maybe it takes the imagination and the sensitivies of an artist to see it; then again, I believe faith makes artists of us all.

PRACTICE FROM A FAMILY PERSPECTIVE

For her book *Our Share of Night, Our Share of Morning,* Rabbi Nancy Fuchs interviewed more than one hundred parents about the intersection between their parenting lives and their spiritual lives. Some were Jewish, some Christian, agnostic, New Age, and otherwise. But all were parents. Where did they feel their parenting and spirituality overlapping? What role did faith play in family life? Can you identify particular times? One new mother describes a powerful sense of "sacred time" she experienced through, of all things, middle-of-the-night feedings with her newborn. A father describes holding his infant child, just rocking and staring, rocking and staring, and knowing that somehow God was in this relationship. From rocking chairs to car rides, the book is full of these moments of subtle amazement. As a parent, it can be so helpful to hear these stories, not only from books but from one another. It can also be helpful to tell them, to be asked to share them. Sometimes it takes such looking back over our own lives to see the grace at work in them.

Another reason to hear and share such stories is that we can learn from one another. We can get ideas, see the deeper possibilities, and even be more intentional about practicing our faith in creative ways. *Our Share of Night, Our Share of Morning,* for example, also describes rituals, prayers, and other activities in which families engage to deepen their lives of faith, as family. The author, a mother herself, describes the excitement she felt as she discovered a practice she could try out with her own family. For example, she discovered one family who, every night at dinner, would hold hands, close their eyes, and say in unison, "Let there be peace on earth and let it begin with us." Very simple, but it was an important ritual to this family.

So at supper that evening, Rabbi-mother Fuchs told her own family to sit down quietly and not to jump up right away and get the ketchup or anything else. She said, "We are now going to hold hands and pray." The family did as they were instructed. Next, in her "most rabbinical voice," she declared that everyone was to find a place of peace inside themselves. She recited the prayerful words and waited "for blessing to descend on the dining room."

And how did the family react? "Instead of blessing," she says, "all hell broke loose." The older child sings, "Let there be peace on earth," in a raucous voice. The younger one whines to get her soup microwaved. Both children leave the table, collide in the kitchen, start yelling at each other. The result: two crying, whining, hungry children and a husband angry at changing the dinner rules with no warning. In turn, our mother-Rabbi ends up crying, too, as her vision of a peaceful world, let alone a peaceful dinner, crumbles in the hands of her own family.

Even under the best of circumstances, to deal with families, especially our own, is to deal with unpredictable, messy, less-than-perfect relationships. After a chapter dealing with religious practices and family rituals, I believe it is important to acknowledge the limits and frustrations when religious life and families collide. Some in the family may resist religion; others may resent it. Some may be deeply motivated; others may be deeply skeptical. Or spouses may come from very different traditions. One may have been raised in a household in which religious rituals were suffocating life and narrowing vision; another may have been raised in a home with nothing. These can be very large challenges to marriages and parenting alike. But when the challenges are big, it is all the more critical to engage them. In other words, the subject of "God" may actually raise more conflict in family relationships before it relieves conflict. Then again, this is the kind of conflict that can be addressed through good conversations and loving care. Conflict around "God" is a chance to hear one another's stories: why one is hostile to religion, why one finds such deep meaning in it, why she doesn't want to go to service, why he does. And so, even through this kind of conflict God lets us see one another in deeper ways.

Rabbi Fuchs says that later in the evening in which her family had their wild, anything-but-peaceful supper, while they were sitting around reading and relaxing later on, they discussed what had happened. She admitted to them that she had been bossy. She had been trying "to prepare, serve, and feed faith" to her children "like homemade, nutritious baby food." She says she had been bossy not only with her family but with holiness itself.

The next thing that happened was a moment of grace, she says. Her daughter pulled off an imitation of her that got them all laughing about the whole affair. The rabbi says of the laughter, "We experienced something larger than ourselves. I had read, prayed, and even preached that 'God forgives our sins,' but I didn't *know* that until I began forgiving my children and they began forgiving me."

LOOKING AT OUR LIVES AS WORSHIP

Look again at this story. What began as excitement over a religious practice led to conflict, which, in turn, led to another kind of religious discipline: confession and forgiveness. Most traditions practice some kind of ritual of confession and forgiveness in congregational worship—prayers of confession, rites of reconciliation, services for atonement. Typically, such practices focus both on our relationship with God and our relationships with others, perhaps even our relationship to creation as well. The reach of confession and forgiveness, though often practiced in congregational worship and life, stretches well beyond. The story from Rabbi Fuchs reveals how congregational practices can reach into family life. They can even teach us how to see our family lives. And, in the spirit of Ethelbert Miller, who sees his life becoming a poem, I am suggesting the possibility of our lives becoming worship.

I am sometimes asked to talk to parents in congregations different from my own tradition of worship. A great way to learn about a community and what it values and how it practices its convictions is to look at its worship materials—often a printed bulletin or worship book of one type or another. Bulletins are great because they typically reveal not only the worship rituals but the larger life of the community from picnics, to youth group meetings, to prayer or social concerns, to what other groups use the building. Talking with parents, I have found the bulletin a wonderful resource not only for learning about their religious community but for taking another look at family life in light of their particular worship practices.

We do a simple exercise. If there is a bulletin available, we look at it. If not, we list the different things that might happen in the community's worship. Usually there are activities such as scripture readings, prayers, music, offering, and sermons. Some congregations have a passing of the peace, confession, and forgiveness. Others have anointing, baptisms, times of silence, cantering, communion, a sharing of joys and concerns, ecstatic dancing, or benedictions. Looking at these activities provides a starting point for discussing religious practices at home, reflecting the concerns of the previous chapter. (For example, could scripture reading happen at home? Could prayer? Talk of God? If these are the religious practices of this community of faith, can the family also be a community of faith? What challenges would this present? What resources could help?)

THE POWER OF GOD AT HOME

But the larger point of the exercise is to take a second look at family life in light of worship. For example, we might look at "confession of sin" and ask, "What's going on with confession in the home? What are your children learning about confessing wrong? What about forgiveness? Is the home a place where forgiveness can happen? Can parents (like Nancy Fuchs) confess to their children? Can spouses and siblings forgive one another? Is pardon given cleanly, or is it withheld and manipulated? Are there limits to forgiveness? Can forgiveness happen without confession?" Because the category is so rich and because home life is so full of the ups and downs of human relationship, parents could spend a year talking about just this one aspect of worship. We are teaching our children spiritual lessons daily in our ways of handling our admissions of failure and through our assurances of grace.

Other examples extend the discussion of practices from Chapter Eight. Consider the connection between the Word of God, the Bible, and our everyday words. Reading the Bible is important for its content, but reading sacred texts also teaches us to respect the power of words in general. So what is happening with words in our homes? Are they used to edify and build up? To teach and guide? Or perhaps words are used more to hurt and to ridicule? Are words used to deceive? Do they tell the truth? There is so much going on when we hear the Word of God, so much learned. But sometimes it takes a second look to notice the connections to our everyday lives.

What connections are there between reading the Word and reading other words? Are words ever read in the home? Could studying scripture and studying homework be related? Historically, Sunday schools, for example, were designed to provide literacy training for those who would otherwise have no other educational opportunities—the poor, slaves in some places, and girls. Students learned to read by reading Bible verses and other religious materials. The connections run deep. Like scripture, can our words be rich with meaning? Maybe we can listen more carefully to our children's words. How might the history of Israel root our own histories? How might God's covenant with a people affect our promises to one another? What connections are there between reading the good news of the

Bible and sharing good stories at home? Consider other kinds of written words as well: thank-you notes and e-mails, letters to friends or to politicians. Or what about the love letters (ever read the Song of Songs?) tucked in the back of a dresser drawer? How might reading, studying, hearing, and praying the scriptures themselves affect our own script? Perhaps a hint of the sacred can rub off. In other words, religious practices and rituals not only shape the rhythms of worship but they can shape the rhythms of our life with others.

Look again at prayer. One of the most powerful understandings of prayer I have encountered is that prayer is attentiveness to God. Given this understanding, how might attentiveness to God affect a parent's attentiveness to children? One mother told of a morning ritual she has with her teenage daughter. They sit together, sipping tea—a kind of adult thing to do but something children often play at, too. They sip tea, have prayer, and just visit. The whole act is a kind of prayer, an attentiveness, face-to-face that will have an enduring impact on both their lives.

What does prayer teach us about praise and gratitude? What is happening with praise in our family lives? Is it reserved for achievement only? Or maybe there is a pervading sense of gratitude for life underneath each "thank you." In a poignant documentary on the Public Broadcasting System (PBS) exploring the moral lives of children, two girls share what it was like living through the riots of South Central Los Angeles a decade ago. The documentary shows some of the everyday dangers they face just walking to and from school. But we also see them playing, relaxing with their mother, and eating meals with their extended family as well. At one point we see the girls in prayer with their mother: "We thank you and praise you that there weren't any killings, or robberies, or drive-by shootings. We thank you and praise you that . . ." As tough as their circumstances could be, watching their lives and listening to their stories a viewer can sense a strength and power and underlying gratitude that gives them a strong place to stand as they face real struggle. It comes through their prayer but also through their smiles and laughter, their studies, their conversations, and their commitment to one another. In the words of the narrator, "You know they're going to make it."

The Power of God at Home

How about tables? Christians can ask, "What connections can we see between the dinner table and the congregational communion table?" For the Jewish community the Passover table is the dinner table. The roots of Christian communion are in this same table, in the Last Supper, which itself was a Passover meal. So the connections are there, historically. But in general parents can ask, "What happens at table? Is there ever time to eat together? Does everyone have a place? Is there room for guests? How is food shared—with each other or with a hungry world?" Reflecting on this, one man extended the discussion of table beyond the meal table to a workbench. He said, "You know that workbench—a table—held some of the most special times I ever had with my own father. I guess you could call it a kind of communion." A lot is going on at table. Some parents, as they think about this, commit themselves to eating one meal together every day. Others, especially those with teenagers in soccer and youth group and you name it, commit to one meal a week; or maybe they commit to making an early breakfast their time at table. Table-time is not only bodily nourishment but soul-time. The table gives a place and time for talking, visiting, sharing, joking, even fussing or crying. These are key ingredients to life in communion with others.

Music and hymns—what other kinds of praise, joy, or singing are going on in family life? What are the chants, refrains, and choruses? What are the anthems? For many people, singing or playing music in their own families as they grew up was foundational for their religious lives. (These people are often our organists and choir directors in congregations today.) One father spoke about his own morning routine of getting up to the alarm bells, then waking his daughter by singing a little song. He got all excited as we explored the connection to his church's worship service, saying, "I never thought of it before, but this is our home version of the church bells calling us to worship, then having the opening hymn praising a new day."

Recall that Kierkegaard called faith a kind of "transparency" to the power that makes us. This look at worship in relation to our family lives is an exercise in transparency. Can we see through ourselves, our lives together, to the glory of God? With a little prompting, people see through to all kinds of beauty and grace. Maybe there is a connection between the water for bathing and the waters of baptism. Perhaps the oil rubbed on a baby's skin is a kind of anointing. Maybe the routine of washing a cut, bandaging it, and finishing with a kiss is a kind of service of healing. Can tumbling on the floor with our kids be akin to rolling in the aisles? Can we pass peace to each other? What happens with offering? What do our children learn about our use of talent and money? What are the creeds? What is the mission? What might the sabbath itself, a time set apart, teach parents and children alike about rest? Is there time to express joys and concerns?

' Or consider blessing. In my tradition, we close worship with a benediction, a "good word," a blessing. One Presbyterian father revealed that, like most parents, before he goes to bed at night he checks on his children. Every night he gently places a hand on each child's head and says (sometimes just thinks), "God bless you." Occasionally they even hear him; usually they are asleep. But I am betting that there is a connection between this nightly ritual and these children knowing, even at subconscious levels, they are loved. What a gift to know you are a blessing.

These are just a few examples gathered from parents taking another look at their lives in the light of congregational worship practices. They represent a depth to home life that has been there all along. Just hearing this father's connection between blessing his children and the benediction in his church has enriched my own simple experience of telling my children goodnight or kissing Jane goodbye as one of us leaves the house. But in noticing the connections, not only is family life seen with depth, so is congregational worship. Each realm becomes more meaningful. Hearing his connection, benedictions at church are more meaningful now, too; they have taken on more texture. Parts of life are connected by a greater whole.

NURTURE AND LEARNING

Over 150 years ago, New England theologian and pastor Horace Bushnell wrote a watershed book for the relationship between family life and religious learning. *Christian Nurture* argues that home and family life could themselves be "means of grace." To say that family life could be a means of grace is to say that families and their everyday lives could be agents or vessels for revealing God's love. As we notice where the deep patterns and practices of faith occur in the midst of home and family life, we are noticing where grace is at work.

Bushnell was particularly concerned about the treatment of children. On the one hand, some leaders in his day misguidedly used the notion of fallen humanity as a license for cruelty. Being of the devil, the logic went, being children of wrath, some thought it warranted to "beat the devil" or "beat the hell" out of children for the sake of their own salvation. Discipline was a major preoccupation. This is one kind of cruelty to worry about. On the other hand, Bushnell noted another kind of mistreatment that he called "ostrich nurture." Referring to the Book of Lamentations (in the King James translation), "Even the jackals offer the breast and nurse their young, but my people has become cruel, like the ostriches in the wilderness. The tongue of the infant sticks to the roof of its mouth for thirst; the children beg for food, but no one gives them anything" (4:3–4).

Ostrich nurture means that no one cares about the children. That could be parents, but it could be a community or even a society, as Lamentations illustrates. According to Bushnell, such lack of care and attention not only damages the body but it damages the mind and soul of children as well.

But the reverse could be true; even simple bodily care—feeding a child, for example, or kind physical treatment—could be means of grace. If the soul is a temple of the Holy Ghost, Bushnell suggests, then the body will be as well. The soul, body, and mind are tightly connected in this theology in a manner, I believe, helpful for parents as they raise and care for their children. In a sense, religious education begins before we are even aware of such distinctions as body, soul, and mind. The life of the body, the life of the mind, and the life of the soul are all inextricably interwoven. Our children are temples of the Spirit of God—the Spirit who binds together body, soul, and mind.

Distinctions between these realms exist, too, but when you are a new, sleepy parent getting up in the middle of the night to feed a hungry child, it can make a difference knowing that you are feeding

the baby's soul, that you are laying the groundwork for spiritual learning, that communion is happening. A man named Chuck reflects on
4 A.M. feedings with his newborn. "We would link eyes and it could
last a half hour or more," he reveals in an interview with Nancy
Fuchs. "I had always suspected that on some deep level, I was fundamentally alone in this world. But now I knew I was wrong. Being together with my child was the realest thing I had ever known." Again,
through the eyes of people like Chuck, we can see a deep continuity
between the grace that can be known in family life and the grace revealed in the larger community of faith. Even the most basic tasks can
be more meaningful than we can say. "God was here in the space
linked between our eyes, in the relationship, the encounter." Interwoven are the love of God and the love in families, even if seen dimly
at 4 A.M. feedings.

ATTENTION AND LEARNING

How amazing that the sheer linking of eyes could be so powerful between a child and a parent. How elegantly simple paying attention is,
but how meaningful. Attention is the key to care and attachment:
being there, holding, seeing, tending, listening. We are made to attend to one another, to attach, to care.

At one level, attention and attachment are matters of survival.
Unlike most mammals, human beings do most of their maturing outside the womb. We pay close attention to our babies to ensure their
existence, to make sure they are safe, fed, and protected from threats
in the environment. Smiles, cries, a sense of wonder, concern, sensitivity, and emotional attachment keep us connected and, from an evo-
lutionary point of view, enable the survival of our species. While other
creatures survive by having quantities of offspring (a fish or turtle may
lay millions of eggs so that a few will survive), human beings have
made it through nurture and care. And the principle instrument of
nurture and care is attention.

At another level, attention and attachment are fundamental, not
only to care but to learning. At first, attention may serve sheer physi-

cal, bodily survival, but human beings do not live by bread alone. We live by meaning, we live by sources of love and hope, we live by a moral and spiritual direction. Without these, frankly, we will not survive as a species; we will kill each other off. But attention is key here as well. Not only do parents pay attention to children but children pay attention to parents as well; by doing so, children learn. As one natural historian puts it, "Parents and their care become the environments in which their children develop, the finishing schools of their brains." Attachment and attention are the first courses in this school. The same capacity to pick up cues and signals from caretakers extends to the larger environment. The child can attend to a bigger world and take it in. As a child learns to walk, the child explores new territory, attending to rooms, houses, yards, and more, sometimes to the dismay of the concerned parent. Children, as they grow and learn and explore, become sensitive to larger and larger dimensions of the world. In fact, in another place I have described learning itself as "the deepening of sensitivities to life," in order to express the relationship between learning and paying attention.

As the child matures, learning gets even more complex. Children engage a world wider yet—a world full of symbols and symbol-systems such as letters, words, or numbers. But learning doesn't stop there. Learning involves sensitivity to even larger realities. Life with others—whether one's family, congregation, nation, or planet—involves learning whole systems of communication, behaviors, and patterns of living. Not only do we learn words, we learn how to speak to others, how to treat others, what is important now, and what is ultimately important. Body, mind, and soul—attention and attachment pervade all levels of learning from smiling, to learning to care for others, to learning God is attached to us. Spiritual learning and teaching, then, involve paying attention to the ways faith works through our lives with one another, a deepening of sensitivities to grace.

Robert Coles, in his book *The Moral Intelligence of Children,* describes the long walks he and his father took together as he was growing up. "He'd share with me—he'd share so very much with me." As Coles describes these walks, he reveals how much he learned, how much he learned about who he is and what is important. These walks were so deeply formative for him, he says, that he cannot even imagine himself being the person he is without having had them. Coles himself has written many books about children, poets, storytellers, and families. He has traveled all over the world interviewing people face-to-face, listening to their stories, their ideas, their words. He often walks with children as he interviews them. This pattern of traveling about and listening to people's stories is beautifully reminiscent of his own long walks with his father. Looking at the connection between these two parts of his life reveals a kind of poetry at work.

For the most part, the kind of learning that happens between children and parents is very undramatic. That makes it a tough sell in our age of hyper-marketing and extreme everything. Just some walking and talking, a little time together, is a rather unimpressive curriculum. "He told me of people he had known, those he liked and did not like and why." Yet Coles explains that these were not monologues descending one way from above. "I followed suit, told him of my buddies, the pals I liked, the guys I didn't like, and why. Later on, naturally, there would be girls I'd mention, even as he'd meet them." What makes a person good? What makes a person not very good? What is valued? What is not? When exploring this territory with those who first smiled at us, first held us, first nursed us, learning is power. "His understated phrases always had great weight for me—such a contrast with all the daily hype that afflicts us these days," Coles reflects. The levels of subtlety on which a child picks up should give us pause. Even "understated phrases" carry meaning, value, and a commentary on modern hype. And this is precisely the level of learning that can and does happen in everyday family living. The attentiveness between parent and child, initiated with clinging and cries, with smiles and food, can be cultivated into adulthood through walks and talks, with sharing and listening. Body, mind, and soul work together.

A Parent's Prayer

The ingredients important to nurture turn out to be important to learning: listening, sharing, respecting, guiding, modeling, telling stories, sharing memories and hopes, and spending time—lots and lots of time. These are ingredients of the life of faith, too. If prayer is indeed a kind of attentiveness to God, to the sacred, to life itself, then maybe learning too is a kind of prayer. Maybe nurturing children in the power of God's securing love is teaching them how to pray without ceasing.

May our children know God's love.

THINKING ABOUT
HOME AND FAITH

QUESTIONS FOR REFLECTION

The following discussion questions are provided to use among groups
of parents, couples, families, and others concerned with raising and
caring for children in faith. They are designed to stimulate discussion.
Some are designed for parents and some for discussions among parents and those working with or concerned about children more generally.

   If you are leading a discussion using these questions, realize that
some could, by themselves, take up the entire discussion time if engaged very deeply or among many people. You will want to pick and
choose among the options. Ideally, these questions will lead to your
own, better questions and to the concerns that come from your own
situation.

CHAPTER ONE   PAYING ATTENTION

1. Can you think of a time when you learned to see another fami-
    ly member in a deeper way? What happened? What opened
    your eyes? How did it affect your relationship? What do such
    experiences teach us about the nature of learning itself?
2. What are your reactions to some of the how-to helps for par-
    ents? What have you found helpful? Do you share the author's
    sense of guilt or resentment with any of it?
3. Why were you named as you were? If you are a parent, why did

you name your child what you did? Have you struggled with changing your name?

4. How do your own children or those close to you seem to learn best? How did you learn best as a child? By doing? Studying? Being disciplined? Playing? Watching? Some combination? How much did your learning depend on your interest in the subject?

5. How do you see the knowledge of God affecting self-knowledge? How do you see self-knowledge affecting knowledge of God?

6. Who are some wise people in your own life? What have you learned from them?

7. Where have you seen spiritual power?

8. Describe a time when you learned from a child.

9. Can you imagine yourself as a spiritual teacher? As a religious educator of your own children? If so, what helps you do so? If not, what gets in the way?

10. When you think about the subjects of family, home, or children in relation to the Bible, what do you think of? If you don't know the Bible very well, what would you guess the Bible's large concerns might be? If you do know the Bible well, how would you summarize its concerns about home, family, and children?

CHAPTER TWO   THE STORY OF HOME

1. Have children said or asked you anything that just paralyzed you? How did you handle it? How do we know when to provide answers to big questions and when to let things be or to say, "I don't know"?

2. Do you think of God as everywhere? Somewhere particularly? Are there places where you believe you sense or have sensed God's presence more intensely?

3. What do you know about your own ancestors or where they are from? In what ways has this knowledge (or lack of it) affected how you think about yourself?

4. How does reflecting on God's creation affect your own thoughts and imagination? What parallels do you see between God creating the universe and people creating homes?
5. What are some of your family stories about surviving tough times?
6. Have you tended to think of faith more as a journey or as dwelling? When or where is each image particularly helpful?
7. Have your children begun asking why questions about religious practice? Do you have stories to tell that might help them understand?
8. What does the sanctuary where you worship mean to you?

CHAPTER THREE   AT HOME AMONG MORTALS

1. Where do you see injustice happening in our world? How does it relate to the use or abuse of power? Where is injustice particularly intense for children?
2. How do you handle the tension between teaching children to be open and kind to others on the one hand but to watch out for themselves and protect themselves from harm on the other?
3. Does this chapter's description of idolatry make sense to you? What are other kinds of idols? What do they do to our lives? What idols do you worry about your children being drawn to?
4. How have children changed your identity? How have marriage, friendship, or being a member of a congregation affected who you are?
5. Describe your first "temple." What would it mean if it were destroyed?
6. What other parallels are there between the life of Jesus and the history of Israel?
7. Do you have any family rituals (such as the grandmother and granddaughter baking bread) that reflect both sadness and hope? Why might these be important for children?
8. What does it mean for God to be at home among mortals?

CHAPTER FOUR   AN ABUNDANCE OF MEANING

1. Have children asked you "meaning" questions about religious practice or anything else? How have you responded?
2. Katherine Paterson's parents read the Bible "not to make us good," she says. What do you think of this? Don't we want the Bible to teach our children to be good? What is the relationship between knowing who we are and the moral life?
3. Do you have any visible treasures (like a pocket knife) reflecting an invisible relationship to an ancestor? What does it mean to you?
4. What does this statement from the chapter mean: "God's love empowers a parent's love and reveals how ultimately meaningful love is"?
5. Do you agree with the chapter's concerns about consumerism and technology in relation to children and family life? Why or why not?
6. What are some more examples of "manufactured dissatisfaction" and of "meaningful dissatisfaction"?
7. Describe a time when you felt an intense sense of wonder or "radical amazement."
8. What are some implications of recognizing the mystery of families? The mystery of a child? Try substituting the word *children* for *people/families* in the quote from Dykstra. How does that affect the way you think about children?

CHAPTER FIVE   WHAT GOES WRONG?

1. When you were a child, how did you learn to think of sin? Breaking commandments? Something we are born doing? How does thinking of sin as twisting something good square with your own understanding of sin?
2. Can you think of kinds of sin or evil that do not fit well with the categories of escapism, idolatry, or manipulation? Would you create another category or other categories altogether?

3. Why might starting a discussion of sin with a description of the image of God be important? What else could being made in God's image involve or imply?
4. If you have, how have you addressed sin and evil with children? What makes it difficult? What helps such discussions?
5. Can religion or spirituality really be sinful itself? What do you make of such an idea? What implications do you see for your own religious life or that of children?
6. Do you recall when the finality of death became real to you? How old were you, and who died?
7. The chapter suggests that an insecurity born of the fragile nature of life is at the heart of sin and makes sin so tempting. Would you agree? Why or why not?
8. Keeping in mind both the strengths and dangers of these patterns, what did you learn about *closeness* and *distance* in relationships as you were growing up? To what extent are you passing on the same patterns with your own children, and to what extent are you changing such patterns?

CHAPTER SIX   FROM FEAR TO COURAGE

1. What kinds of things scared you as a child that an adult might not have realized or appreciated? Where did you find comfort and security?
2. Name some particularly anxious times in your children's lives. Did change or transition play much of a role, or was something else at work?
3. When have you heard the divine "sing" through a simple deed? Was it something someone did for you? Something you did for someone?
4. What are some simple things that help your children know they are loved?
5. What are children learning about the lovability of others who are outside your home or family?
6. Explore the statement, "Individuality can feed family life;

family life can feed individuality." Can you provide any concrete examples of this?

7. What are some of the struggles you have faced negotiating the tension between individuality and community in your own family? In your congregation?

8. In what ways is your family creative? In what ways are your children creative?

9. What cultivates security and courage for children? What cultivates "ultimate security"?

CHAPTER SEVEN   WHAT'S IN A HOME?

1. How did you answer the questions posed in the exercises of this chapter?

   A home is _____?

   A family is _____?

   My definition of home did not include _____?

   My definition of family forgot _____?

2. How difficult was it answering them?

3. Tell a story about what your family means to you. What does home mean to you? Are there any experiences that particularly reveal what family or home means to you?

4. What's in your recipe?

5. How would you describe love?

6. Try asking these questions of your own children. How did they answer?

7. What other implications do you find in the descriptions of ancient households?

8. How difficult would it be for your congregation to incorporate some form of "family impact" analysis or reflection into its programming? What other questions, besides the ones posed in this chapter, could it include?

9. How did you answer the questions about meaningful experi-

ences in a congregation? How do you think your children or congregation's children would answer them? Try asking them.

Chapter Eight   The Joy of Practice

1. Identify a time when you practiced something you enjoy (for example, a musical instrument, a new language, lines for a play, a dance step, an athletic skill, an artistic skill) in order to learn. How does it compare to the author's experience of drumming? What connections do you see between your experience and practices of faith?

2. What does it mean for faith to be a general orientation to life? How do you think your life or your children's lives might be different if faith were not important to you?

3. If you were to create your own list of faith practices, what would be on it?

4. If you were to identify three or four strengths in your own family life, what would they be? How could you build on them for religious practice? What are one or two practices you have thought you might like to do but you were not sure how to go about them? What would help your family be able to try?

5. What practices, if any, have you tried with others or alone that have gone well? What has not gone so well? What can be learned from these experiences?

6. What does prayer mean to you? Meal-time? The Bible? How would your children answer these questions?

7. How difficult do you find talking of God in your home? Is it easier somewhere else?

8. Identify some opportunities for you and for children to practice service and caregiving beyond the home or congregation.

9. Identify a time when you had an all-out, cut-loose time of joy or celebration with your children. Was it planned? Spontaneous? Some of each?

10. How do you understand the statement that religious practices are the "somewheres" in home life that help us sense the sacred everywhere?

CHAPTER NINE   SACRED CONNECTIONS

1. Can you describe a particular sense of "sacred time" you felt with a child?
2. Do you have your own "let there be peace on earth" story?
3. What meaningful rituals or activities have developed in your household (that may or may not be explicitly part of your faith life)?
4. You may want to do the exercise described in this chapter. If so, either use a worship bulletin or list the various components of worship in your tradition or congregation. Simply explore where a version of these might be happening in your own household.
5. What other connections do you see between attention and attachment? Between attention and learning?
6. Who were your significant moral guides when you were growing up? What kinds of subtleties do you believe you picked up on from them?
7. What prayers do you have for your children?

REFERENCES

CHAPTER ONE   PAYING ATTENTION

The idea of educational "connoisseurship" is drawn from Elliot W. Eisner's *The Educational Imagination* (New York: Macmillan, 1985). I also tell a version of the story about Cora saying "me" in *The Texture of Mystery: An Interdisciplinary Inquiry into Perception and Learning* (Lewisburg: Bucknell University Press/London: Associated University Presses, 1998), p. 106. The Calvin quotes come from his *Institutes of the Christian Religion* (Philadelphia: Westminster, 1960), edited by John T. McNeill and translated by Ford Lewis Battles (I.I.1 and I.I.2). The story from Anne Lamott comes from her book *Bird by Bird: Some Instructions on Writing and Life* (Anchor Books, 1994), pp. 18–19. Norman Maclean's reflections are found in *A River Runs Through It and Other Stories* (New York: Pocket Books, 1976), pp. 2–4.

For the story of Ruby Bridges, I am relying on Robert Coles's descriptions in his book *The Moral Life of Children* (Boston: Houghton Mifflin, 1986), as well as his description in the video *Listening to Children: A Moral Journey with Robert Coles* (Social Media Productions and PBS Home Video, 1995). Disney also aired a made-for-television movie, *The Ruby Bridges Story,* on January 18, 1998, on ABC. Ruby's prayer and the quote from her mother are from the children's book by Robert Coles: *The Story of Ruby Bridges* (New York: Scholastic, 1995).

An excellent summary of some of the nineteenth-century debates about the Sunday school can be found in H. Clay Trumbull's 1888 *Lyman Beecher Lectures Before Yale Divinity School.* These are published as *Yale Lectures on the Sunday-School* (Philadelphia: John D. Wattles, Publisher, 1888), Lecture IV.

Trumbull himself supported the Sunday school but articulated well the arguments and concerns regarding it.

CHAPTER TWO   THE STORY OF HOME

For those more interested in the history and development of the Bible itself, there are plenty of resources available in libraries and bookstores or on the Internet. Many Bibles (for example, *The New Oxford Annotated Bible,* New Revised Standard Version [New York: Oxford University Press, 2001] or *The HarperCollins Study Bible* [New York: HarperCollins, 1993]), as well as standard encyclopedias, explain the differences between translations, as well as the differences between the Bibles of different religious traditions.

The quote from Calvin is from his *Institutes of the Christian Religion* (cited in Chapter One), I.XII.14. For a discussion of more ways in which the creation is dependent on God's presence, see Jürgen Moltmann's *God in Creation: A New Theology of Creation and the Spirit of God* (San Francisco: HarperCollins, 1985), especially pp. 86ff. Moltmann's work has deeply influenced my own on this issue, especially on the connection between "void," "nothingness," and "God-forsakenness." For a deeper discussion of the way in which a "part of God," in a sense, wanders with the displaced Israelites, see Jürgen Moltmann, *The Trinity and the Kingdom* (San Francisco: Harper & Row, 1981), pp. 25ff.

On the connection between promises and family life in the quote from Craig Dykstra, see his book *Growing in the Life of Faith: Education and Christian Practices* (Louisville: Geneva Press, 1999), p. 98. The point from Wendy Wright comes from her book *Sacred Dwelling: A Spirituality of Family Life* (New York: Crossroad, 1989), p. 12. The quote from Abraham Heschel is from his book *Israel: An Echo of Eternity* (New York: Farrar, Straus & Giroux, 1967), p. 11.

CHAPTER THREE   AT HOME AMONG MORTALS

The quote from Diana R. Garland comes from her book *Family Ministry: A Comprehensive Guide* (Downers Grove, Illinois: InterVarsity Press, 1999), p. 317. The story about a grandmother and granddaughter baking bread comes from

Nancy Fuchs's *Our Share of Night, Our Share of Morning: Parenting As a Spiritual Journey* (HarperSanFrancisco, 1996), p. 175.

On the ways in which God meets forsakenness with presence, I refer again to Moltmann's *God in Creation,* especially pp. 86–93 (cited in Chapter Two). The story from John Westerhoff comes from his book *Bringing Up Children in the Christian Faith* (San Francisco, Harper & Row, 1980), p. 3.

CHAPTER FOUR   AN ABUNDANCE OF MEANING

The quote from Katherine Paterson comes from her book *The Spying Heart: More Thoughts On Reading and Writing Books for Children* (New York: Lodestar, 1989), pp. 45–46. The quote from Walter Brueggemann is part of a larger discussion about the connection between wisdom and the world in his book *Creative Word: Canon as a Model for Biblical Education* (Philadelphia: Fortress, 1982), p. 73.

Regarding the impact of consumerism on family life, a very important book is Christopher Lasch's *Haven in a Heartless World: The Family Besieged* (New York: Basic Books, 1977). Regarding the impact of technology and its deleterious effects on attention, as well as on family and social life generally, I am deeply indebted to the work of Albert Borgmann, especially *Technology and the Character of Contemporary Life: A Philosophical Inquiry* (University of Chicago, 1984) and *Crossing the Postmodern Divide* (University of Chicago, 1992). A more generally accessible rendering of Borgmann's thought is Richard R. Gaillardetz's book *Transforming Our Days: Spirituality, Community and Liturgy in a Technological Culture* (New York: Crossroad, 2000).

The descriptions of the Holy come from Rudolf Otto, *The Idea of the Holy* (London: Oxford University, 1923), pp. 5, 12–13. The story of the children hearing about Aslan comes from C. S. Lewis's *The Lion, the Witch, and the Wardrobe* (HarperTrophy edition, 1994), pp. 67–68. The discussion of wonder and radical amazement can be found in Abraham Joshua Heschel, *Man Is Not Alone: A Philosophy of Religion* (New York: Farrar, Straus & Giroux, 1951); the quotes are from pp. 12 and 16. Some of the experiences of wonder, as reported by students, I also discuss in *The Texture of Mystery,* p. 203 (cited in Chapter One).

On mystery, see Gabriel Marcel, *The Mystery of Being* (Lanham, Maryland: University Press of America, 1950), Vol. 1, pp. 211ff.; the example of the sleeping child comes from pp. 216–217. On Marcel's illustration of the family as a mystery, see his essay "The Mystery of the Family" in *Homo Viator: Introduction to a Metaphysic of Hope* (New York: Harper & Row, 1965). One of the best and most accessible renderings of Marcel's description of mystery (and which was my own introduction to Marcel's work) comes from Craig Dykstra's *Vision and Character: A Christian Educator's Alternative to Kohlberg* (New York: Paulist Press, 1981), pp. 34ff.; the quotes come from pp. 36–37. Dykstra beautifully draws out ethical as well as educational dimensions of mystery.

The story about Joel is in Kathleen Deyer-Bolduc's devotional book, *His Name Is Joel: Searching for God in a Son's Disability* (Louisville: Bridge Resources, 1999), pp. 113–114.

CHAPTER FIVE   WHAT GOES WRONG?

I have greatly simplified Edward Farley's analysis of sin in *Ecclesial Man: A Social Phenomenology of Faith and Reality* (Philadelphia: Fortress, 1975). Farley suggests two fundamental categories of sin: *flight* (which I have renamed *escapism* here) and *idolatry,* with *manipulation* being a subcategory or a form of *flight* (see *Ecclesial Man,* Chapter 6). As a counterpoint to sin, redemption, according to Farley, has a double-sided character: freedom *from* manipulation and determination by others but also a freedom *for* others—caring and obligation to others (see pp. 160–161). There is a rich history of the idea of this double-sided character of sin and freedom, especially in the tradition of nineteenth-century philosopher Søren Kierkegaard. The quote from Kierkegaard and the description of *flight* are taken from his work, *The Sickness Unto Death,* translated and edited by Howard V. Hong and Edna H. Hong (Princeton: Princeton University Press, 1980), pp. 63ff.

The quote from Jürgen Moltmann is taken from *God in Creation* (cited in Chapter Two), p. 11, in a discussion of the "community of creation." The story about "childcare in the desert" comes from Ernest Boyer Jr.'s experience that he tells in his book *A Way in the World: Family Life as Spiritual Discipline* (San Francisco: Harper & Row, 1984), p. xi. The quote regarding the dangers of unchecked individualism in society come from the book by Sylvia Ann Hewlett and Cornel West, *The War Against Parents: What We Can Do For America's Beleaguered Moms and Dads* (Boston: Houghton Mifflin, 1998), p. 96. The quote connecting compassion and parenting is from p. xiv. *The War Against Parents* is an excellent book for insight into the ways in which a society—its culture, legislation, economy, and government policies—can line up to work against parenting, which, as the authors demonstrate, is to work against the well-being of children.

Salvador Minuchin describes the *disengaged–enmeshed* continuum in his book *Families & Family Therapy* (Cambridge: Harvard University Press, 1974), pp. 54ff. The quotes come from pp. 55–56.

Chapter Six   From Fear to Courage

Katherine Paterson won the prestigious Newbery Medal for *Bridge to Terabithia* (New York: Avon Books, 1977). The quote from Paterson is taken from an address she gave at Louisville Presbyterian Theological Seminary on November 13, 1999, as part of the *Faith, Families, & Congregations* conference hosted by the seminary's Center for Congregations and Family Ministries. The story and quote from Wendy Wright are taken from her column "Sacred Dwellings" in *Family Ministry: Empowering through Faith* (Vol. 13, No. 4, Winter 1999), p. 8.

One of the best discussions of courage from a theological perspective is Paul Tillich's *The Courage to Be* (New Haven: Yale University Press, 1952). The quotes from Tillich come from the titles of his Chapters Four and Five. The whole discussion in this chapter of courage is informed by Tillich's understanding of courage, which itself has roots in Søren Kierkegaard's analyses of anxiety, despair, and faith itself. The quote from Kierkegaard is from *The Sickness Unto Death* (cited in Chapter Five), p. 49.

The story from Anne Lamott appears in her book *Operating Instructions: A Journal of My Son's First Year* (New York: Fawcett Columbine, 1993), pp. 69–70. The quote about sacred deeds is from Abraham J. Heschel, *Between God and Man: An Interpretation of Judaism,* a collection of Heschel's writings edited by Fritz A. Rothschild (New York: Free Press, 1959), pp. 80 and 86.

The quote from Robert Coles also comes from the video *Listening to Children: A Moral Journey with Robert Coles* (cited in Chapter One). The quotes from Jürgen Moltmann and the discussion about the "song of creation" come from his book *The Way of Jesus Christ* (San Francisco: HarperCollins, 1990), p. 289.

On the dangers of "hurrying," see David Elkind, *The Hurried Child: Growing Up Too Fast Too Soon* (Reading, Mass.: Addison-Wesley, 1981).

CHAPTER SEVEN   WHAT'S IN A HOME?

The description of ancient family households in the Bible relies on and quotes from the chapter by Leo G. Perdue titled "The Israelite and Early Jewish Family: Summary and Conclusions," in Leo G. Perdue, Joseph Blenkinsopp, John J. Collins, and Carol Meyers, *Families in Ancient Israel* (Louisville: Westminster John Knox, 1997), pp. 175–176. The description of Roman households of the early Christian era relies on and quotes from the book by Carolyn Osiek and David L. Balch, *Families in the New Testament World: Households and House Churches* (Louisville: Westminster John Knox, 1997), Chapter 1, generally, and pp. 17, 25, and 33, specifically. Judd Hendrix is the local pastor I quote who at the time was working for and describing the approach to family ministry by Second Presbyterian Church of Louisville, Kentucky.

To date, the most recent version of a "family perspective" by the U.S. Bishops can be found in *A Family Perspective in Church and Society* (Washington: United States Catholic Conference, 1998). This document also advocates the use of "family impact" questions when planning programs and making policies in churches. One of the best resources for considering the implications of family ministry as a perspective in congregations is Diana Garland's *Family Ministry: A Comprehensive Guide* (cited in Chapter Three).

The description of the Boston-area synagogue comes from Brita L. Gill-Austern's chapter titled "The Braid of Generations: A Model of Family Ministry," in the book *Tending the Flock: Congregations and Family Ministry,* K. Brynolf Lyon and Archie Smith Jr., editors (Louisville: Westminster John Knox, 1998). The quotes come from pp. 62–63 and 58–59. This book is an excellent resource for reflecting on and designing strategies for doing family ministry in congregations; it profiles approaches to family ministry in a wide variety of congregations.

See Mihaly Csikszentmihalyi and Eugene Rochberg-Halton, *The Meaning of Things: Domestic Symbols and the Self* (Cambridge University Press, 1981) for a description of their research into the meaning of home. The quote comes from p. 139.

CHAPTER EIGHT   THE JOY OF PRACTICE

General background for this chapter includes the discussion of practices in Craig Dykstra's *Growing in the Life of Faith* (cited in Chapter Two), especially Chapters

REFERENCES

4 and 5. See also *Practicing Our Faith: A Way of Life for a Searching People,* edited by Dorothy C. Bass (San Francisco: Jossey-Bass, 1997), as well as Alasdair Mac-Intyre's *After Virtue: A Study in Moral Theory* (University of Notre Dame, 1981) and Albert Borgman's two works cited in Chapter Four, *Technology and the Character of Contemporary Life* (especially Chapter 23, "Focal Things and Practices") and *Crossing the Postmodern Divide* (especially the section "Focal Realism" on pp. 116ff. and the section "Hyperreality" on pp. 82ff.).

Several authors pose various lists of historic practices or forms of activity, standing beneath the list I have proposed for families. In addition to Dorothy Bass's and Craig Dyskstra's works cited earlier, see for example, John Westerhoff's *Bringing Up Children in the Christian Faith* (cited in Chapter Three); Maria Harris, *Portrait of Youth Ministry* (New York: Paulist, 1981), or her *Fashion Me a People: Curriculum in the Church* (Louisville: Westminster/John Knox, 1989); Gordon W. Lathrop's *Holy Things: A Liturgical Theology* (Minneapolis: Fortress, 1993); and Margaret R. Miles's *Practicing Christianity: Critical Perspectives for an Embodied Spirituality* (New York: Crossroad, 1988).

The quote from a child about God as her parents' parent comes from Robert Coles's *The Spiritual Life of Children* (Boston: Houghton Mifflin, 1990), p. 129. Based on hundreds of interviews with children, this is one of the best works available illustrating the constructive and meaningful role that spiritual life plays in the lives of children. It also illustrates the powerful role both homes and congregations play.

The discussion of the role of meals and equality in early Christianity and Judaism relies on *Families in the New Testament World* by Osiek and Balch (cited in Chapter Seven), especially Chapter 8, and on the book by Don Browning, Bonnie J. Miller-McLemore, Pamela D. Couture, K. Brynolf Lyon, and Robert Franklin, *From Culture Wars to Common Ground: Religion and the American Family Debate* (Louisville: Westminster John Knox, 1997), particularly Chapter 5. The relatively few places in the New Testament that would seem to promote inequalities or even slavery, many scholars believe to be compromises made for the sake of survival in a threatening culture. (See, for example, Browning and others, pp. 147–149, for a discussion of the issues.) Admittedly, this is very difficult to prove one way or the other.

The research on meals out of Columbia University is reported in "A Weapon in the War on Drugs: Dining In," by Joseph A. Califano Jr., LL.B. This is an article on the Web site of The National Center on Addiction and Substance Abuse at Columbia University (www.casacolumbia.org). According to the Web site, this editorial was originally published on October 19, 1998, in several newspapers.

The reflection from Marian Wright Edelman comes from her book, *The Measure of Our Success: A Letter to My Children and Yours* (Boston: Beacon Press, 1992), p. 4. The story from James McBride comes from his book, *The Color of Water: A Black Man's Tribute to His White Mother* (New York: Riverhead Books, 1996), pp. 50–51. For a "strengths approach" to family ministry, see Diana Garland's *Family Ministry* (cited in Chapter Three), especially Chapters 8 and 14.

CHAPTER NINE   SACRED CONNECTIONS

Ethelbert Miller's quote is from an interview from "The Diane Rehm Show" on National Public Radio August 8, 2000. Currently, the interview can be heard through NPR's Web site. Miller was discussing his beautiful book, *Fathering Words: The Making of an African American Writer* (New York: St. Martin's, 2000). The quotes and references from Fuchs's *Our Share of Night, Our Share of Morning* (cited in Chapter Three) are from pp. xvi–ii, 4, and 12. The story of the girls in Los Angeles comes from the documentary *Listening to Children: A Moral Journey with Robert Coles* (cited in Chapter One). Coles is the narrator quoted. I thank Chip Andrus for the example about church bells and call to worship.

Two sources, in addition to some of the practices literature listed in Chapter Eight, stand behind the exercise of looking again at home life in light of worship: Gordon Lathrop's *Holy Things* (cited in Chapter Eight) and an address given by Thomas Long at the Louisville Institute's conference, *Practicing Christian Faith: Interpreting the Contexts, Strengthening the People,* September 26, 1997, at Louisville Presbyterian Theological Seminary. Neither focuses on home or family life particularly, but each makes connections between worship life and other dimensions of living that gave rise to the exercise. Wendy Wright's *Sacred Dwelling* (cited in Chapter Two) works in a similar vein, connecting parts of a home to theological themes and ideas (rather than worship per se).

The quote from Horace Bushnell is taken from *Christian Nurture* (Grand Rapids, Michigan: Baker Books, 1979, reprinted from the 1861 Scribner paperback edition), p. 272. Bushnell describes "ostrich nurture" in Part I, Chapter 3, and he describes how physical nurture is to be a "means of grace" in Part II, Chapter 3. The natural historian (and writer) quoted is Susan Allport, who discusses the general importance of attention, attachment, and love in humans in Chapter 9 of her book, *A Natural History of Parenting: From Emperor Penguins to Reluctant Ewes, A Naturalist Looks at How Parenting Differs in the Animal World and Ours* (New York: Harmony, 1997). The quote is taken from p. 171.

On learning as a "deepening of sensitivities," see my book *The Texture of Mystery* (cited in Chapter One), especially Chapter 15, "Sensitivity to Life." The reflections and quotes from Robert Coles come from his book, *The Moral Intelligence of Children: How to Raise a Moral Child* (New York: Random House, 1997), pp. 187–188.

THE AUTHOR

J. Bradley Wigger teaches Christian education at Louisville Seminary and directs the seminary's Center for Congregations and Family Ministries. He is a Presbyterian minister and has worked variously as a social worker in a special education school, as a congregational pastor, and as a stay-at-home father. He received his Ph.D. from Princeton Theological Seminary and has written several articles and book chapters in addition to his 1998 book, The Texture of Mystery (Bucknell/Associated University Presses). He is currently the associate editor of and a regular columnist for the journal Family Ministry: Empowering Through Faith. He is coeditor, along with Diana R. Garland, of the Families and Faith book series published by Jossey-Bass.

INDEX

H

Habitat for Humanity, 124, 142

Harris, M., 179

Hebrew Bible, 26, 27

Hell: definition of, 28; descending into, 53

Hendrix, J., 178

Heschel, A., 38, 71, 72, 79, 103, 149, 174, 175, 177

Hewlett, S. A., 84, 176-177

His Name Is Joel (Deyer-Bolduc), 74–75, 176

Hitler, 67

Holidays, 146. *See also* Celebrations

Holiness, 28, 69–71, 72, 175

Home: among mortals, 41–59; connection between God and, 24–25; defining, 114–117; expansion of, 62; and faith, thinking about, 165–172; meaning of, finding, 125–127; mystery of, 75–76, 115; piety of, 91–92; relationship between congregations and, 113, 117–121, 126, 133; significance of, 1–2; spiritual elements in, 113–127; story of, 23–39

Hope: expression of, 45, 46, 47; glimpse of, 57; loss of, 51; seed of, 29

How-to material, 3–4

Humanity, creation of, in God's image, 79–81

Humility, 89, 90, 134; hushed, 70, 71

Hurried Child, The (Elkind), 108, 177

Hurrying, 108–109, 133

Hymns, 35, 157

I

"I Wonder as I Wander" hymn, 35

Idea of the Holy, The (Otto), 69, 175

Identity and learning, 6–8, 10, 11, 145

Idolatry, 42, 78, 85–88, 91, 101, 176

Idols, 45, 73, 85, 86, 100

Implied promises, 31

Inadequacy, parental, feelings of, 4, 16, 17, 18, 113

Individual autonomy, emphasis on, consequences of, 84, 91, 176

Individual dignity, 91, 104, 107

Individuality, 9, 11, 104–105

Injustice, 43, 45

Insecurity of life, 92–94, 104

Integrity, community, 107

Interplay between part and whole, 104, 105–106, 107

Inter-relatedness, 91

Isaac, 32, 33

Isaiah 6:3, 28

Isaiah 65, 45, 58

Isolationism: national, 93; religious, 120

Israel (Jacob), 32, 33, 34

Israel, origin and history of, 25, 26, 27–39, 41–59

Israelites, 25

J

Jacob (Israel), 32, 33, 34

Jerusalem: fall of, 44, 55; hope for, 45; new, 58; return to, 46–48; significance of, 52; the temple in, 38, 44, 46–47, 48, 55, 56, 118; Wailing Wall of, 56

Jesus: aspects of, 49–51; crucifixion of, 51–52, 53, 55; on family relationships, 120; on mealtime, 139; resurrection of, 52–54; significance of, 56

Jesus–Crucifixion–Resurrection, 49–55

Jewish religion. *See* Judaism

Job, 48

John, 49

John 2:19–22, 55

Jordan, crossing, 36, 38

Joseph, 33–34

Joshua, 38

Josiah, 44

Joy: place for, creating, 135; and play, 147; of practice, 129-149

Judah, 42, 48

Judaism: Bible in, 26; braiding the generations in, 121, 122, 123; early, households of, 117–118; movement within, 49; and persecution, 118; significance of land in, 33. *See also specific religious activities/practices*

189

193

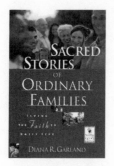

Sacred Stories of Ordinary Families:
Living the Faith in Daily Life

Diana R. Garland

$19.95 Hardcover

ISBN: 0–7879–6257–0

Beautifully written and lyrically told, Diana R. Garland's *Sacred Stories of Ordinary Families* identifies resilience, strength, and faith in the stories of all kinds of families, motivating parents to think about how faith shapes their own family lives.

Drawn from Garland's extensive interviews with 110 families, these stories give voice to families—not just "traditional" first-marriage and biological-children families, but also single-parent families, remarried and blended families, single adults, and older married and widowed adults. Connecting these stories with the Christian story and with biblical texts, Garland explores the diversity of structures these families represent and the ways they seek to live their faith in everyday life.

The rich diversity of families in *Sacred Stories of Ordinary Families* allows the book to resonate with readers of all backgrounds. Readers will be encouraged to connect their own experiences with the sacred and to tell their own stories of faith—to one another and to the congregational community. Grounding their understanding in biblical stories and themes and finding a resource for their own faith in coping with everyday stress and major crises, readers will come away from the book with a stronger sense of how they, too, are living the faith.

Diana R. Garland is the chair of the Social Work Department at Baylor University and director of Baylor's Gheens Center for Christian Family Ministry. A published author, she is also editor of the journal *Family Ministry*. She resides in Waco, Texas, with her husband, David.

[Price subject to change]

Seasons of a Family's Life:
Cultivating the Contemplative Spirit at Home

Wendy M. Wright

$19.95 Hardcover

ISBN: 0–7879–5579–5

Wendy Wright has written a revelatory book about family life. So often taken for granted, so often dis-counted as drudgery, in her gentle but skilled hands the life of the family is transformed into spiritual reality. As she probes the dish-washing, car-pooling, diaper-changing, curfew-setting reality of everyday life she guides us to sacred ground.
—James P. Wind, president, the Alban Institute

In *Seasons of a Family's Life,* highly respected writer Wendy M. Wright offers a reflective, story-filled examination of the spiritual fabric of domestic life. It focuses on the cultivation of spiritual awareness amidst the ordinary drama of family life and challenges families to wrestle with the great religious questions which have always been part of our human quest: Who in fact *am* I? What is a life well led? What is most essential? What is my responsibility to others? How do I deal with evil? What constitutes the good?

Wright has a particular gift for combining a deep seriousness of pur-pose, a poetic use of language, and a great sense of humor. With this approach, she explores family life as a context for nurturing spiritu-al practices, providing parents with suggestions for developing con-templative practices in the home. Each chapter is a lesson in being attentive to the wonder of our experience in family, glimpsing the sacred amidst the chaos of our daily lives.

WENDY M. WRIGHT is a popular speaker at retreats, workshops, and conferences, and a professor of theology at Creighton University. Wright is a frequent contributor to *Weavings* and *Family Ministry,* and is the author of eleven other books. She and her hus-band live in Omaha, Nebraska, and are the parents of three young adults.

[Price subject to change]